EDUCATION FOR DEVELOPMENT
Social Awareness, Organisation and
Technological Innovation

Education for Development,
Social Awareness, Organisation and
Technological Innovation

J.M. Heredero

Manohar
1989

First Published 1989

ISBN 81-85054-82-7

© J.M. Heredero

Published by
Ramesh Jain
Manohar Publications
2/6 Ansari Road, Daryaganj
New Delhi-110002

Lasertypeset by
Microtech Advance Printing Systems (P) Ltd.
H-13 Bali Nagar, New Delhi-1100015

Printed in Indid at
Lancer Press
A-3/1 Maya Puri-I
New Delhi

FOREWORD

November 1963: a new Jesuit Father fresh from the University of Chicago arrives in Ahmedabad, in Northwestern Gujarat state. Born in October 1929, he had joined the Society of Jesus at the young age of 16 and when he was 20 he had left his native Spain for India. Much of the long Jesuit training still lay ahead: the study of Philosophy, Gujarati, Theology. When, finally, in 1962, the Jesuit training was completed, a secular degree was still required to be able to teach in government-approved schools. So he was sent to the States to obtain it. The University of Chicago was a good corrective to the anti-intellectualism reigning in the circles where this young Spaniard moved. The intellectual rigor and academic discipline of the University of Chicago left its mark on him. Pure theory, it is true, bored him; but so did pure activism. Metaphysics did not attract him; but neither did activity devoid of transcendental meaning.

November 1963: this young man is appointed lecturer of Political Science: a big classroom full of newcomers to the College whom he has to teach the Indian Constitution. Most students are not interested. Small groups in the higher classes face an outdated syllabus of four political science papers. Occasionally some bright students want to learn: teaching becomes such a joy! But most are not interested.

Giving up one's own family, fatherland, freedom to end up teaching some irrelevant subject to students who are not interested. Is there meaning in it? Is there meaning in religious life, after all? Two disquieting questions: who is an educator? What is religious life? Pure theory would not bring peace to this young man. Flitting in and out of the classroom amid smiles of approval from his students was not enough. Deep down there was emptiness, because he saw no meaning. This cannot be education, no matter how loudly the system proclaims the contrary - not so loud, after all: cynicism was rampant in academia.

And what is religious life? Of course, he knew the answers. But pure theory would not quieten him down. He found it so attractive and yet so incomprehensible to see his religious confreres at peace with themselves and the whole religious system. Did they see meaning in it? "The problem with you", he was told, "is that you think too much". Old Rousseau had said it already. Thinking makes man depraved. May be they were right, after all: less thinking and more acting. He went in search of a Guru, an Indian Jesuit who taught him how to pray, how to feel the presence of God deep down in his heart. That was not theory; but an experience. But it was not an empty activity, either. There was a new vision: reality goes well beyond the material objects which our eyes see, our hands touch. Reality is difficult to express in words our lips utter and our ears can hear. And yet, there are words which point heavenward. What is love, what is justice, what is peace, what is fellowship and, in the end, what is a human relationship? The New Testament did convey a message which did not make things easier - all that Christ said about poverty and the poor challenged this young priest's new found spirituality.

True, there were poor students in the College, there were students belonging to the Scheduled Castes, as well. Actually, a number of them had come to him in search of advice. The culture and values prevalent in the student population made them feel like fish out of water in these surroundings. They were spending money beyond their means on clothes and entertainment in an effort to be like "them". They hated to be what they were; they wanted to be - high caste. Sheer impossibility. But one could always pretend. Some actually did with greater or less success. But deep down, there was always fear not so much of being found out (of course the high caste knew) but of being rejected even in this new avatar. They were poor: was this their "natural habitat", did they really belong here? This was a posh locality, the richest families in town sent their children to this college; its annual functions and fairs drew huge crowds. The whole place reeked of sophistication and, may be, snobbery.

This young priest did not object to the Church's presence in higher education. In fact, he was all for it. His question was: why can't all these immense resources be made available to the deprived masses? It was not a question of a cheap, symbolic gesture to appease a sense of guilt. The issue was not guilt but meaning. Did this college make Christian sense, if its resources were not made available to the dispossessed where, according to the Gospels, Christ did manifest himself? In other words, the college had to make a contribution as a college in order to remain a Christian college.

This contribution must evidently be a specialized educational venture, say, in the rural areas where real education is rarely given. Surely, such a prestigious college could organize an educational programme which would help the rural poor and help the college to remain in touch with the realities of the country. What was the use of teaching economics, sociology, political science, botany and biology if all these disciplines did not take cognizance of the real India? Needless to say, relevance could not easily become reality. But one thing could certainly be achieved: to prevent the college from becoming so identified with a small section of society as to turn increasingly irrelevant to the rest of the nation.

Twenty-five years later, the same priest, no longer young, looks back at the same college, at the Centre he helped to establish and at the work done in the villages. Critical at times, understandingly involved most of the time, he tries to re-create the dream and the reality.

ACKNOWLEDGEMENTS

This book would not have been but for the Department of History, Temple University, Philadelphia. I am thankful to Dr. David R. Davis, chairman, for the facilities provided to me to spend several months working in the Department. The real inspiration behind this book is Dr. Howard Spodek of the same Department. It was he who suggested that I spend my sabbatical at Temple, he who made the arrangements, he who motivated me to write the book, and finally, he who took upon himself the task of going through the manuscript over and over again painstakingly annotating each page with his queries, comments, suggestions and corrections.

Special thanks are due to the secretarial staff of the Department – they provided all the material facilities, specially the use of the computer which facilitated so much the preparation of the manuscript.

Here in our Centre, Dr. Sarvar V. Sherry Chand prepared the final draft. Her quiet but efficient editing made it possible to have the manuscript ready within the stipulated time. Shri Astad Pastakia helped update Chapter 5. Many others have also gone through the manuscript and given their suggestions: Dr. Barbara Joshi, Dr. Suguna Ramanathan, Dr. Robert Hardgrave and Dr. Eleanor Zelliot. To all of them my thanks.

Finally my thanks to the publishers who have taken so much interest in the book and have brought it out so promptly.

JM Heredero

INTRODUCTION

The present book is a sequel to *Rural Development and Social Change* which describes the efforts of a group of college professors, who moved out from urban college premises to rural areas in a novel answer to their educational calling. This marked a change from formal to non-formal education, from just teaching to joint learning, from the professor's chair to the group's inner circle.

Ten years have elapsed since that book was published. The educational thrust has continued unabated – but dramatically modified by that eventful happening which is real education. First, a need was felt to move from the city to the villages. To understand a new reality one must become part of it: learning demands *immersion*. Later, the overpowering influence of the structures was clearly felt. A moneylender can teach more effectively than well-meaning, kind-hearted, urban professors. Warmth elicits warmth, but helplessness determines behaviour. No change in the structures, it became clear, meant *no new* learning. The dilemma could not be eluded: either cease to be real educators or become social activists.

The college professors then took up a new function, that of trying to change structures. What did that mean? A political struggle to capture state power in order to transform society? Or was our society open enough to new structures? Was a new system of production – leading to a new set of social relations – possible without a revolution? It did seem possible at the micro level.

The vision was clear: the implementation, difficult. Without heightened social awareness, a new production system could not come into existence. Without a new socio-economic structure, keen social awareness would lead to pain and frustration: direct political struggle is an unequal fight in the case of the scheduled castes.

A new system of production, a new system of education, a new type of teacher who teaches as he *does*, all this was a dramatic departure from the earlier educational efforts of the former college professors. "Doing" requires knowledge of agriculture, forestry, organisational development, financial management – all these are areas in which technical expertise is essential. At the same time, the new system of production demanded a set of values − technical knowledge for social justice − which need not necessarily be the in thing at our IIMs and IITs from which technical expertise is usually drawn. It was difficult to find such technical experts; and yet a Technical Wing did come into existence to help the old Educational Wing.

The vision was clear: social awareness would help restore self-respect, and give the poor a new faith in themselves, an understanding of the need for unity and cooperation which would energise their community into action; in the process, the community would develop its organisational power. Social justice cannot be given; it must be won. Eternal vigilance is the price of justice. But no matter how it may be sought, social justice cannot be achieved without a struggle. The present book is the story of such a struggle − a picture of light and darkness, hope and foreboding.

Chapter 1 sums up the pedagogy followed earlier and explained in the previous book and then goes on to examine how this pedagogy was modified as a result of continued interaction with the people. Chapter 2 presents a picture of the geographical area where the Centre has been working. Chapter 3 describes the beginnings of the work in this area and Chapter 4 goes on to examine cooperativism as the main instrument in both educating and changing the system of production. Chapter 5 lists the achievements of the new cooperatives; Chapter 6 evaluates the movement as a whole. Chapter 7 sums up and draws the main conclusions from the whole experience.

The book is based on a very concrete experiment. It is neither armchair philosophy nor a presentation of pure facts; but attempts to explicate a theory of education on the basis of practical experience. It deals with an all-India problem: poverty and social discrimination. It details the importance of organisation and explains the role of knowledge − be it social, scientific or technological − in the fight against injustice. The present study explains the answers given in a concrete situation. But the issues raised are of national importance.

Finally, the experiment described here is the work of a team and not of a single individual. Many have been working at this task, all of them members of the Behavioural Science Centre on the campus of St. Xavier's College, Ahmedabad. Some remain, others have left while new ones have joined. The strains and stresses of development are felt equally, both by those who are supposed to be helped and by those who mean to help. Growth and progress require courage to let go of the past and to face a new situation as new. What was good yesterday may become irrelevant tomorrow. This book has tried to portray this reality as objectively as possible. But man is fallible. His actions must be constantly criticised. It is in this process of action and reflection that man attains excellence. The experiment presented here with candour expects criticism from its readers: a dialogue which may help all of us to attempt more creative and constructive solutions to the problems which vex our nation.

April 1989   J.M. Heredero
Ahmedabad

CONTENTS

1

THE BEHAVIOURAL SCIENCE CENTRE: COURSES TO BACKWARD CASTES

The initial educational efforts of this team are narrated in a book published ten years ago (Heredero, 1977). The book explains the limitations under which this team laboured:

Our approach to rural development has been determined to a large extent by our own limitations. We are college teachers, and our profession has made us exclude a number of possible approaches to rural development. Obviously we cannot be full-time social workers and be all the time with the people. We have also refused to organise developmental schemes for the people because we think that would be incompatible with our work as educators. For one thing, running aid-giving schemes would mean giving much of our time to administration, which would distract us from our educational work. Moreover, it would identify us in the eyes of the people as aid-givers and that would make it difficult for them to see us as educators. (p. 4)

The book (p. 5) describes first what the team understood by rural development:

Economic and technological development do not necessarily mean real development. The latter takes place when there is personal growth, which means increased *awareness* . . . .

Our approach to development is based on our understanding of rural society. In it even more than in an urban setting, it is the community which really matters. The individual has little meaning apart from the community. In fact, attempts to help him outside the community can be dangerous not only because the chances of success are very small, but also because we may do much harm to the individual in question . . . .

Our approach is also based on our understanding of education. It is certainly not the type of formal education imparted in our schools and colleges — that covers only a very small fraction of man's reality. Education should enable a person to deal more effectively with others, with his work, and also with himself (his needs, his feelings, his motives, his past history). . .

Education is a creative act and an educated man is a creative man. It is in this area that technology is used to impart education. Thus to apply somebody else's agricultural technology to one's own fields requires much more creativity than we are accustomed to think . . .

A truly creative act is not the outcome of intelligence alone. Feelings and the imagination play a very important part as well. That is why in our training we pay much attention to this aspect. Finally, the introduction of new ideas in a village requires courage. That is why it is important to train not just one individual but a whole group. They can support, encourage, and be a source of ideas to one another.

Briefly stated, the team's understanding of its role in rural development is (p. 8):

. . . non-formal education given to a group of 30 persons taken from, and representative of, the same village community. The aim of this education is the whole man: his feelings, needs, motives, his intelligence and, if necessary, his spiritual powers. The ultimate purpose is to increase the participants' awareness and to prepare them to be more effective in dealing with the other members of the community, and with their own work.

The pedagogy followed is summed up in the following paragraphs (pp. 74-75):

1. *Defreezing*. The initial stages are marked by embarrassment, shyness and even suspicion on the part of the participants. Therefore it is necessary to break the ice. This is done by engaging them in external, absorbing activities . . .

2. *Warm interpersonal support* . . . a climate of trust is created between trainers and participants and among the participants themselves . . .

3. *Faith*. The cornerstone of our courses is faith. . . The effort is to make them aware of their own latent powers and thereby increase their self-confidence.

4. *Cooperation* . . . It is important to clarify their ideas as to the meaning of cooperation and have it tested in actual practice by engaging them in activities where their cooperative spirit will show.

5. *Decision-making*. Before the course ends. . .they make some [decisions] for themselves individually and for the village as a whole.   This implies giving them information mostly about agriculture.   .about banking, government schemes and agro-industries and practical information about decision-making with suitable exercises to put it into practice.

6. *Final choice*. The participants . . . set individual and group goals . . . . They do this after taking into consideration the various options open to them and other factors. . .

7. *Follow-up*. For some time the trainers offer their services to keep up the spirit of the group by visiting the village.

Although the initial participants in this course belonged to the high or middle castes, by the end of the third year several attempts were made to take participants belonging to the scheduled tribes and castes (Heredero, 1977: 78-95). The new participants made the Centre realise the inadequacy of its pedagogy and, therefore, the need of the new one described in this study. There is an obvious continuity between the earlier work of the team and the pedagogy followed today by the Centre (as the Behavioural Science Centre will be called hereafter). But there are also fundamental differences which must be pointed out. The first marks a departure from the American trend (Bradford, Gibb, Benne, 1964; Schein, Bennis, 1965; Egan, 1970) characterised by group dynamics and sensitivity training with its emphasis on feelings, the "here and now" and individual

awareness, towards the Latin American approach of social
awareness which stresses society and its structures (Freire,
1972, 1973; Smith, 1976). The former approach relied much more on
a set of artificial conditions (the so-called laboratory method)
contrived to elicit expression of feeling and, ultimately, insights into
oneself and others. It relied heavily on what was happening in the
group itself which the participants were taught to observe; these
observations gave matter for personal feedback on each participant.
The new approach, without altogether abandoning this practice,
places much more emphasis on social awareness: "What is
happening in your village, how does it affect you all, what are the
forces behind all these events, what can one individual alone do?"
Activities and exercises were used much more in the earlier
approach: the new one relies more on dialogue concerning injustice
and exploitation which, the trainers know, are an overriding concern
with the participants.

Another important departure was in the recruiting policy. It was
thought that caste people could afford to pay educational consultants
to teach them. The Centre, therefore, decided to concentrate all its
resources on the education of those who could not afford to pay –
the tribals or the former untouchables.

The new educational approach was adopted for the first time in
1974 with a group made up exclusively of "ex-untouchables." It was
striking to see how easy it was to organise the immense knowledge
they had about their own situation into a coherent pattern which
pointed so clearly to the causes of the social evils. The trainers did
nothing but suggest the various headings under which they could
narrate their experience of being exploited:

Economic injustices: Moneylenders have to be paid exorbitant
interest rates; sometimes we have to work for the Rajputs
without pay; we have to pay heavy penalties when our cattle stray
into their fields, but when their cattle enter our fields nothing is
paid to us; some of our people are still bonded labourers for all
practical purposes; the wages paid to us by the moneylenders are
very low; when they make us work as share-croppers in their
fields, they make us bear the expenses and they take away all the
benefits. In the end, we have to borrow money from them and
thus remain deeply indebted.

Social discrimination: The way they treat us, the words they use, everything they do with us shows contempt: they do not give but throw things at us; tea is served in earthen vessels (their own would be defiled by us); our elders must use the honorific plural even when addressing their children, while their children may use the disrespectful singular to address our elders; we can't cycle in their presence, we must get down and walk; they object when we wear decent clothes; the very words used to describe us have a pejorative meaning; those of us who are in the village panchayat are made to sit on the ground while the Rajputs sit on chairs . . .

Political discrimination: The Rajputs are hand in glove with the bureaucracy, their requests are granted by government officers be they policemen or revenue officials; they contrive to win the elections and, therefore, the Member of the Legislative Assembly, the MP, the district and taluka panchayats are all in their hands; they see to it that money and other benefits from government schemes accrue to them; even when meant for us, they will not give them to us, unless we pay a bribe; if we complain to the police, they just won't listen to us; even the opposition parties are not very different . . .

The criterion of self-respect and group unity to fight the injustices perpetrated against them by the higher castes was now the aim of the courses. Given the prejudices against the former outcastes, the only unity one could hope for at this moment was that of the latter among themselves. Greater equality would be required before the unity of all the poor could be contemplated.

Social awareness and the fight against injustice were the dominant themes in our courses from 1974 to 1977, when another important departure from the previous courses and from the Centre's educational approach took place. As long as it remained totally dependent on the high caste moneylender, a small minority could not fight effectively against injustice. A change in the economic structure itself was absolutely essential. And, consequently, the courses had now a very concrete goal: to *unite* the former untouchables in a *cooperative economic venture* which would free them from the clutches of the moneylenders. Self-respect remained a priority and so did unity; social awareness was still the main tool to awaken self-respect and to unite the group. But much more stress was now laid on the impact that society had on individuals and groups; and, consequently, on the need to change those conditions which, like economic overdependence, precluded a life of dignity and self-respect.

In other words, a change had taken place in the Centre's understanding of education. Formerly the Centre had believed: "Change the people and *they* will change society." Now the Centre asserted, "No lasting change in our trainees can be expected, unless the socio-economic structures which condition them are changed." The change sought was in the mode of production itself. The cooperative would enable our participants to be both owners and workers. This would enable them to become self-sufficient and thus free themselves from the high castes. This departure made the Centre change from an educator who runs courses into an educator who learns with the people how to run a cooperative, how to cultivate wastelands, how to deal with the bureaucracy, and so on. The educator who is constantly learning is entitled to teach.

As for agricultural technology, the Centre now realised that mere knowledge of agriculture was not enough: managerial skills, and financial resources were two other essential elements required to achieve any important breakthrough. It would be impossible to make all these things available to individuals; but through the cooperative the required mobilisation of resources could be achieved for the whole group. Here again a change in the mode of production was the aim, that is, from a feudal one, characterised by low productivity, to a modern one.

The courses are now the introduction to a more important and more lasting educational process which takes place in the cooperative. They are meant to create awareness of the spirit, the ethos and the new culture required to bring about the proposed changes. The cooperative itself is more like a school where all the cooperators learn new skills, qualify to perform higher tasks and discuss the day-to-day problems which the community faces.

To sum up: the Centre's pedagogy moved from efforts to "motivate" the participants (McClelland, 1961; Heredero, 1968; McClelland, Winter, 1969, Alschuler, Tabor, McIntyre, 1970), to sensitivity training and t-Groups (Bradford, Gibb, Benne, 1964; Schein, Bennis, 1965; Egan, 1970) and from the latter into education aimed at raising the social awareness of the participants (Freire, 1972, 1973; Smith, 1976).

The two former approaches presuppose an experience of society where the individual does have some power; while the latter looks at that section of society which is deprived, in which individuals are not even sure of their means of subsistence, let alone the possibility of shaping society.

The New Pedagogy in Practice

According to the new policy, only tribals or those from a backward caste are accepted into this educational programme. The Centre has been very active in the tribal belt along the eastern border of Gujarat state (see Appendix 2) and in the Bhal region of Kheda district. When either a tribal group or a scheduled caste from a village asks to attend a course (usually because the people have heard of us from others or because they have seen the work of the Centre) an educational officer from the Centre moves into their village, explains the goals of the course and asks the elders to have as many adults as possible attend the course. Not all the men can be absent from the village in far away Ahmedabad for ten days; but a representative from each household can. It is important that all the sections or factions of the village be represented. Otherwise, the information received and the decisions taken may, in the long run, work against unity.

All lodging and boarding expenses in Ahmedabad are defrayed by the Centre. Travelling expenses, however, must be met by the people. Having the courses in Ahmedabad is more expensive; but it has many advantages. It makes the group acquainted with, and less afraid of, the city; it stresses solidarity between the urban and the rural population. The city is a retreat setting for the villager who is far removed from the daily worries and concerns of his usual milieu. A course in the village would mean distractions. Other villagers would be passing by and would pause to observe what is going on. Our participants' attention would be divided, one eye on the group and another on the passersby. In the strange surroundings of Ahmedabad the participants easily coalesce into a team; the trainers, their only link with an apparently hostile environment, are more easily accepted as full members of the group. It is also easier to act in new ways in new surroundings, away from the inevitable ridicule on the home turf; both trainers and trainees learn faster in such an atmosphere.

On the other hand, the courses now focus more sharply on social structures and their impact on both the individual and the whole *jati*. A short introduction of each individual and a detailed enquiry into his main concerns opens the course. A boisterous game in which everybody takes part helps to *defreeze* them and to make everybody feel at home. Their behaviour in the game is later analysed and reflected upon. Questions of leadership are discussed: was there a front man? A technical hand? Who was the real leader? Their attitudes towards victory and defeat and the emotions attached to them may be examined after the belligerence of the game – the emotional outbursts of joy among the victors and anger among the vanquished – subsides to normal levels.

An elaborate decision-making game takes up most of the second day. Planning, cooperation, managerial skills, leadership qualities are all tested and discussed as variations of the game are tried. By now the groups feel more at home, less self-conscious, more vocal and attuned to this training method.

A review of the previous days sets the ball rolling on the third day and lets the trainers judge whether the group is ready to launch into the deep. If so, a slow, concrete and methodical analysis of their own village begins:

Who owns how much land, cattle, equipment, houses – figures and names are jotted down on the board by one of the trainers. What is the position of the Vankars vis-a-vis the big landowners? How are they treated as labourers . . . . Much as it has been described earlier.

The facts and figures mentioned are invariably challenged by some, defended by others, and discussed by all until a consensus emerges. One instance of ill-treatment recalls the memory of many others which are also narrated to the group. A pattern becomes visible, unwanted yet unavoidable. The elders become restless and defensive, the young indignant. The trainer quietly asks, "Is this fair? Is this just or moral?" The defensive attitude of the elders is opposed by the unequivocal moral condemnation of the youth – elderly hesitance gradually yielding to youthful certainty.

The trainers quickly sum up the analysis so far made; and then the final question is asked which hurts but leads people to a higher stage of awareness: "Do the high castes have regard for you?" The thousand and one ways in which they are slighted, the subtle and crude ways in which they are despised, all erupt thunderously as from a long dormant, suddenly active volcano.

The trainer makes them reflect: "It is bad enough if others despise you: but are *you* going to despise yourselves, your own brothers and sisters?" The session may end dramatically with a solemn oath to respect one another at all costs. Self-respect now becomes the *leitmotif* for the rest of the course.

Caste ideology is taken up on the third day. The previous session had made an appeal to the emotions; it had tried, by arousing anger and indignation against the exploiters, to exorcise a misplaced and oppressive sense of guilt. The gains made in the heart are subsequently strengthened with a cool, logical and scientific appeal to the mind — a plain, down-to-earth, epistemological discourse on the origins of knowledge.

Words are coined by others and language itself is given to us ready-made. Indeed there are many languages on earth, all made by men.

The understanding that man has both of himself and of society differs considerably from place to place. It has been fashioned by learned pundits, all high caste. Poor, illiterate people had nothing to do with it; it has been given to them by other men; it is all the creation of man.

Self-interest biases understanding. The bias of the high caste shows up in the meaning and values they have invented for the poor. Bias, not malice, is emphasised. The blame should not be laid so much on persons, themselves the victims of circumstances, as on those things which enslave man, like money and greed, power and lust for it. "Unless this point is grasped," it is facetiously added, "tomorrow the Rajputs will need help to free themselves from the Vankars."

The Socratic method of questions and answers is best suited to clarify ideas. Still, a good story adds colour to the dialogue.

Once upon a time there was a very good man in a big village of the Bhal. He was rich. He had 200 acres of land, 20 pairs of bullocks, 40 servants, and many cows and buffaloes. He had a six year old son, innocent, intelligent and alert. Another boy, slightly older, used to work in the garden. He was well-behaved and, on occasion, would take care of the son who became very fond of him. The servant was a Vankar. One day the son asked his father, "This servant is so kind-hearted, he is so hard-working and yet he wears such poor clothes. I asked why the other day, and he told me that his wages did not allow him to buy better clothes. Why doesn't he receive a better salary?"

The story is suddenly interrupted, there is a short silence and a question is shot at the listeners. "What will the father answer? What *can* he answer?" Of all the answers they attempt, they soon realise, the most practical one is the slanderous stereotype. "Oh, these people are lazy, they are dirty, no matter what we do for them they will spend the money on drink. And, by the way, you shouldn't mix much with him or else you too will become like him."

To establish the motive is an important element in criminal proceedings. It makes sense to our listeners; so much sense that they may start talking among themselves oblivious of the trainers who, sensibly, withdraw.

The new epistemological insights enable the group to take the bull by the horns — caste ideology: its meaning and values, the way it imbues language, culture, religion and social relations. It is a slow, lengthy but rewarding exercise.

Caste Ideology

A serious fight against casteism demands a serious study of caste ideology and the role ideology plays in the formation of everybody's subjectivity. At some stage or other, the Centre's educational approach includes its study.

Ideology has been studied from two very different angles: the conventional approach has always been the study of *ideas*. This is the case with ideologies in political science, in religious movements or, in cultural anthropology, the ideologies of an ethnic group. R.S. Khare (1984) applies this method in his study of the ideology of the Chamars (a group of ex-untouchables) in Lucknow. Marx, on the other hand, propounded the theory that all ideologies are ways of legitimising injustice. His analysis, however, does not explain how ideologies are still upheld much after a communist takeover has radically changed the previous socio-economic structures. Althusser and the Euro-communists (Therborn, Poulantzas, Debray) have refined ideology to a concept which goes beyond *ideas* to include all those things which form the subjectivity of a human person. The Centre, interested not in ideas alone but in human behaviour, has found Therborn's formulation very useful in understanding and explaining caste ideology (see Appendix 1). What follows is meant to explain the manner in which these ideas are conveyed in an actual educational programme.

What is caste ideology? is the first question put to the course participants. The answer will be something like this:

It is a belief that castes are arranged hierarchically according to the principle of purity. It is a belief that one is born into a higher caste because of one's good deeds in the previous birth. Similarly, sinful acts are the cause of one's birth into a lower caste. . .and those born outside the pale of caste are so impure that they defile others.

It may not be easy for them to say the last words and yet it is important that they accustom themselves to enunciating the belief of the high castes, courageously.

Ideologies, the trainers explain, deal with meaning and values. Caste ideology explains the meaning of existing inequalities and, in the process, makes us value and esteem a Brahmin and despise a Harijan. And this is accepted by all of us. Why? How does this process take place?

Tne process, the trainers themselves answer, *begins* at birth. Infancy plays a critical role in forming the subjectivity of individuals, specially as far as the unconscious is concerned.

"How are small children taught the values of caste ideology?"

"That is all they see in the village. We teach them to fear the high castes. They see the way they treat us . . ."

"And what about *their* children?"

It may take some time for the participants to give concrete examples. But the story of the rich man, narrated earlier, helps them to reflect and realise the number of ways in which a Rajput's child is taught to despise the scheduled castes. And, indeed, it is difficult to understand the extent of caste prejudices unless one takes into consideration the feelings of antagonism and contempt assimilated by the infant unconscious. An Indian sociologist, describing the reaction of caste Hindus to Harijans who assert their rights. remarks: "It is not one of mere economic or political opposition. It is a reaction that touches the raw depths of the historical beings" (Sheth, 1979: 36)

"That is too bad. How can anyone change all this? It has gone so deep into everybody's minds!"

"Well, if we accept defeat," the trainer adds, "do you know what happens to all of us? We become *slaves* of caste ideology. We are tamed as bullocks and dogs are."

The process of *subjection* to caste ideology is then spelt out.

"The values of caste ideology are tamely accepted by us both consciously and *unconsciously*. Values are accepted by us without our realising it, through feelings. Ordinary language makes generous use of words which carry *affective* connotations and are value-laden: words like impure, low, dirty, menial, scavenger, untouchable, illiterate, lazy, poor."

Vernacular words are immediately mentioned by them.

"These words produce feelings of dislike, contempt or even revulsion. Opposite feelings are elicited by words like upper, pure, educated, rich, influential, feelings which make a person feel superior. Gestures and symbols can also arouse our feelings and imagination. Gestures of superiority and contempt towards the other, like making him stand at a distance, sit on the ground. Gestures like throwing things at, rather than giving them to him. These are powerful symbols which convey feelings of contempt. The very arrangement of the village is highly symbolic − the location of your houses outside the village. On the other hand, touching the feet, offering a preferential place to sit, show deference and evoke feelings of respect, appreciation or admiration."

"Such words, gestures and actions breathe the values of caste ideology. Like breath, those values are not argued about, they are just taken in."

This may be enough for one session. In the next, the role of ideology in legitimising unjust socio-economic structures is emphasised. This is done in three consecutive steps:

First step. Caste ideology does much harm to the poor. The strength − the only power − of the poor is their numerical strength. If the poor were united, they would be able to assert their rights. The rich know this very well; that is why they attempt to "divide and rule." In the Bhal itself, the majority of the people, irrespective of caste, are poor. Their interests are similar. Unity and cooperation would win them political power and would make quick economic progress possible. But, will caste people join hands with the scheduled castes? Never. Death rather than defilement, would soon become a battle cry, and all chances of a united front would be ruined. Caste ideology divides the poor and prevents them from prospering.

The ultimate reason for this state of affairs is that the lowest castes are constantly treated with contempt and end up by believing that they are inferior to the others. On the other hand the upper caste poor think that they are superior and thus refrain from uniting with the other poor. They remain entirely in the hands of their caste leaders. Were they to join hands with all those whose economic plight is the same, they would both free themselves from their leaders' tutelage and even become leaders themselves in a new movement. Caste ideology blinds them to their own possibilities.

And then appealing more directly to their own experience, "What was your position thirty years ago? At that time everybody accepted untouchability. It took an Ambedkar, himself a scheduled caste member, to challenge the old beliefs. Who dares to defend untouchability in public nowadays?"

Second step. Ideologies serve to legitimise existing privileges because they are either invented or explained by pundits or priests or scholars who are all at the service of the rich.

Examples of how ideologies and even religion are made to serve the interests of the rich and powerful are then quoted. Priests used to crown emperors and kings. In Japan the Emperor was, for a long time, thought to be a god and so were the emperors of Rome. Religion is used to protect the powerful; while, actually, the founders of all religions defended the poor. There is a simple explanation of this phenomenon: priests and scholars were helped by the rich and were thus obliged to them. . .

Third step. Some of the concepts basic to caste ideology are taken separately. Thus, for example one of the trainers may say:

"Let us take one concept, the idea of *purity*. You are told that the high castes are pure and the Vankars impure. Now, where do you find more unfairness, injustice, exploitation, downright stealing, discrimination and all the other injustices you have mentioned so many times, among the Vankars or among the Rajputs? Who exploits whom? Is that what religion understands by purity? And a little below the belt: they cannot drink from your cups because you have used them; but what about their illicit affairs with Vankar women?" Hypocrisy must be exposed ruthlessly.

Other examples may then be adduced by the participants themselves.

Summing up: the pedagogy followed impresses upon the participants that caste ideology is a creation of man and helps only the upper caste rich. It must be rejected by all sensible people, specially the poor who suffer more from it. The Indian Constitution has rightly stressed the equality and dignity of all men. It tells us that we are all *brothers*. These are the main ideas which are put across to the participants over a number of sessions. Of course, rigidity is shunned as far as possible. One topic need not be taken up in continuous sessions, it may be interwoven with others. Games may be played either to break the monotony or to stress a point. For example, after explaining the origin of knowledge from society and the absurdities accepted even by intelligent people, the following activity may be taken up (Heredero, 1977: 82): A volunteer is blind-folded. A number of cubes are given to him and he is told, "Your task is to pile them up one on top of the other. When you remove your hands, they must not fall down. Now tell us, how many cubes can you put up?" With a little pressure, there have been instances when an individual brought down his initial estimate of 10 to a mere two!

The obvious question is: "Why did you change your mind?" "Well," comes the answer, "you kept on insisting and I was afraid." The moral is clear: trainers have a position of authority and you believe them. And so do you, when the Rajputs and the pundits and other learned people in society tell you that you are lower than the Rajputs and other high castes.

So far, the main topics have been described. But, apart from the content, the process itself is important as the following example will illustrate:

A solemn oath, it has been mentioned earlier, has been taken to respect each other. For all their good intentions, they are likely to laugh at their colleagues and even ridicule them. When that happens, the proceedings are stopped and a stern question asked: "Didn't we agree to respect each other? Didn't we vow to take our brothers seriously?" This question may have to be asked by the trainers once or twice; soon somebody else in the group will take their place. Self-respect, the notion, becomes now a concrete reality. A new ethos replaces the old: the certainty of acceptance drives away the fear of ridicule. Fearlessness begets joyful involvement and creativity.

The ideas explained so far form the backbone of the course; they are likely to unfold very differently in each group because no two courses are alike. Each one is as unique as its participants. Sometimes the very first session lasts several days, when an issue is brought up by the group, which demands immediate attention: an unresolved conflict which disturbs the group – personal differences, may be; factional fights, quite often; sheer prejudice, most of the time. Worries must be dealt with as they come, or no learning will take place. Peace of mind, peace in the group, is the key to greater awareness. This aspect of the course is, however, very much part of the old approach (Heredero, 1977: 7):

> Education should enable a person to deal more effectively with others, with his work, and also with himself (his needs, his feelings, his motives, his past history). It is a process of growth, a pilgrimage on which the instructors have to accompany the pilgrims. The journey is undertaken by them; the teacher's role is only to show the possible routes to follow, to give encouragement when the going is rough. Education is a dialogue in which most of the talking is done by the people while the teacher listens and tries to understand. On occasion he fosters the dialogue with his questions, and his reflections. Sometimes he feeds the dialogue when he answers questions.

The paths taken may be different; but the end of the journey is always the same: the preparation of an action plan. The group is split into small parties each one preparing its own. The economic problems, the existing social relations, the impact of caste ideology, in a word, their new understanding of themselves and their circumstances is brought to bear on their determination to build a better society. The plan of each party is criticised, necessary changes introduced – or, if it is to the liking of the others, adopted by the whole group. The course is over. Action begins. And so does the real involvement of the Centre. But before turning to the next chapter, let us take stock of the gains.

Fundamentally, the target of the course is the group and its individual members. It does aim at the existing structures, but not directly as yet; on the contrary, the success of the course is possible because its participants have been isolated from the conditions and circumstances prevailing at home. Knowledge, it must be stressed again and again, is conditioned by the circumstances in which we live. It is necessary to take people away, temporarily, from the oppressive circumstances in which they live, to create a new knowledge and awareness. It is an artificial atmosphere, undoubtedly, but one which facilitates new insights, greater awareness and, consequently, the hope of changing society – an entirely different and more arduous task. However, the advantages gained in an artificial atmosphere will be short-lived if similar conditions are not created in actual life. This was our earlier fundamental failure. But failure *after* the course should not blind us to the real achievements *during* the course.

Briefly, the low self-image of the Vankars is effectively dealt with and the seeds of self-respect are sown. Self-blame is replaced by a critical understanding; causes, not symptoms, are perceived. The wonder of mutual support, critical yet unequivocal, lays the foundation of unity and cooperation. The proven ability to express themselves in a group builds up self-confidence. A capacity to look at the whole situation rather than fragments of it – not at mere individuals but what they represent in society – takes root during these days and may yield abundant fruit later on. The iconoclastic realisation that knowledge originates from man breaks the spell of formerly enslaving myths and opens the way to greater awareness and to the possibility of transforming action. All of this is embryonic still but alive and full of possibilities.

At this moment, the role played by the self-image must be brought sharply into focus. As one thinks he is, so he acts. *Possunt quia posse videntur*, chanted Virgil. They can, because they *think* they can. More often, they do not act because they are convinced that they cannot. This principle, like life itself, operates within set limits. No amount of thinking can do away with prison or death. Limiting situations apart, behaviour *is* determined by one's self-image. "I am not good with my hands," "metaphysics is not for me" or "teaching is not my cup of tea" set the course of an individual's life. Similarly, "the Vankars will always be fighting among themselves, they can't remain united. They are like that; they will always remain at the bottom of society" – such beliefs, not fate, *karma* or *kismet* ruin the life of a group. An image, however, may be sheer false consciousness or the result of an experience, the cruel blows of hammer and chisel. Words and deeds, affirmation and sanction, uphold caste ideology. Rebels may reject a current ideology. Their rejection may even serve to uphold that ideology if society punishes them and thus frightens the rest into subjection — affirmation and sanction, the two wheels on which caste ideology marches forth triumphantly even amid unwilling vassals.

In the cloistered seclusion of a training course, groups can easily vow to reject discrimination. In the village, however, it is a different story which must now be told.

2

THE BHAL AND ITS VANKARS

The Bhal

Two regions of Gujarat are known by the name of Bhal. The great Bhal is in the southwestern region of Saurashtra. The small Bhal is in the northwestern part of Kheda district in the Cambay taluka. It is a semi-arid area with a tropical monsoon climate.The monsoon rains are erratic and long dry spells are common during the rainy season which commences at the end of June and lasts up to the end of September.

The soils are generally classified under coastal alluvium. They are deep dark greyish brown in colour and clayey in texture. The water table varies from 2 to 5 metres in depth and the ground water is brackish. Drainage is poor. Tidal sea waters have rendered large tracts of land saline. Wastelands abound near the sea. Until recently, agriculture was poor business. Now a canal from the Mahi river irrigates this area during the monsoon, making paddy cultivation a good source of income.

This is the description of Cambay given by the *Imperial Gazetteer* (IX: 292):

From the position of the State between the Sabarmati and Mahi, both of which are tidal rivers, the soil is so soaked with salt that the water becomes brackish at a little distance below the surface.

Cambay is a gentle, undulating, alluvial plain, without any rock exposure. The fauna does not differ from that of the neighbouring British District of Kaira [now Kheda], though the former presence of tigers in large numbers is said to be indicated by the site of a village named Vagh Talao or 'tiger tank.' The climate is equable, the temperature rising to 108 in May, when the minimum is 75 and falling as low as 46 in January, at which season 84 is the maximum. The annual rainfall averages 31 inches.

Although the percentage of scheduled castes in Kheda district as a whole, is only 6.05 per cent (slightly lower than the 6.8 per cent in the state), in the Bhal area of Cambay taluka the scheduled castes are about one-third of the population; of these about three-fourths are Vankars.

The Scheduled Castes

"Outcaste," "untouchable," "ex-untouchable," "Harijan" (literally: man of God), "depressed class," "exterior caste," are some of the terms used to designate the 100 million, who make up the most exploited section of Indian society. It is not easy to choose the right word. "Ex-untouchable" would be the most appropriate term but for its offensive and derogatory connotation. Scheduled caste is preferred because it is the most acceptable and value-neutral term. However, it is inadequate, since it excludes former untouchables who have changed their religion and who are often more discriminated against than their own caste brethren.

The term "scheduled caste" was first adopted in 1935, "when the lowest-ranking Hindu castes were listed in a "schedule" appended to the Government of India Act for purposes of statutory safeguards and other benefits (Dushkin, 1972: 166). The Constitution of India followed a similar procedure, empowering the President

to specify, after consulting with the Governor of a state, those "castes. . .which shall for the purpose of this Constitution be deemed to be Scheduled Castes in relation to that State. . . ." Once promulgated, this list can be changed only by Act of Parliament.

A Scheduled Castes Order was promulgated by the President in 1950 which basically re-enacted the 1936 list. The major additions were four Sikh castes and the provision for the first time of lists for areas which had none previously (Galanter, 1984: 132).

The term "scheduled caste" is appropriate in the context of the existing legal provisions and government action.

Otherwise it is meaningless. The minority it designates is not a single, undifferentiated group but a huge, diverse population. . .

The members are born into numerous castes (more than four hundred), each of which has its own identity, traditions, and characteristic set of relations with other castes. To treat the hundreds of castes on the list as a single Scheduled Caste category is simply to deal with aspects of a common relationship their members have with governments. (Dushkin, 1972: 166)

This relationship with government, however, is vital. As Leĺah Dushkin (1972: 165) states, "India's system of official discrimination in favour of the most 'backward' sections of her population is unique in the world, both in the range of benefits involved and in the magnitude of the groups eligible for them."

These benefits granted by government can be grouped into three categories: First, government, through several constitutional and other legal provisions, has attempted to remove discrimination against the scheduled castes. Second, there are both general and specific development and welfare programmes to help them.

But the most important help given to the scheduled castes is called the reservation system. The Constitution required the reservation of seats in the legislatures for a period of ten years, which can and has always been extended. It also allows the reservation of seats for scheduled castes and tribes in education and government service. In practice, one out of seven members of the lower houses of the central and state legislatures is a person from a scheduled caste.

Most states also either provide reservations or require co-option of Scheduled Caste members into village *panchayat* councils. Reservations also exist, usually not in proportion to population, for admission to many, though not all, higher educational institutions. Reservations in proportion to population, and sometimes in excess of it, are applied by both Centre and states for direct recruitment and some types of promotional posts in government service; a number of other provisions go along with them. In both education and government jobs, the reserved quotas must be filled by qualified candidates; if there are none available, the seat or the job goes to someone else (Dushkin,1972: 172).

As a result of this policy Parliament in 1967, for example, had 77 members belonging to the scheduled castes out of its total strength of 515 (Joshi, 1982: 181). In the state assemblies out of 3236 MLAs

470 belonged to the scheduled castes (Kamble, 1982: 130). Gujarat's share was small, 11 out of 168 legislators. When the Chief Minister is sure of a comfortable majority in the Assembly, 11 legislators do not have much political clout. But there are times when the balance is so tenuous (due to party infighting) that even one member of the assembly wields power, let alone a group of 11.

The affirmative action on the part of government was necessary because of the social and economic discrimination to which the ex-untouchables were subjected. This paper has already referred to the psychological impact that such discrimination has on the scheduled castes it has also mentioned some of the practices which are prevalent in the Bhal. Dr. I.P. Desai has studied untouchability in Gujarat and lists (1976: 11-24) the following practices:

1. The untouchables have a separate source of water in the village.

2. They are not allowed entry into temples.

3. They are not allowed to enter into a *savarna* (caste people's) house.

4. They are not allowed to enter shops. The shopkeeper does not give the goods into their hands (to avoid physical contact).

5. The Hindu barber does not cut the hair or shave the beard of an untouchable.

6. The tailor does not take the measurements of an untouchable, but stitches his clothes by approximate measurements.

7. The employer throws the wages to the labourer.

8. Untouchables have to step aside while walking on the road, if a caste Hindu appears in the vicinity.

9. The untouchables are made to sit at a distance in panchayat meetings.

10. Untouchable students are made to sit separately at school.

11.   Untouchable students are not permitted to touch the water pots or water storage tanks. They are given water by the *savarna* students. There may be separate glasses for them and water may be poured out in them or it may be poured into the untouchables' cupped palms. Or they may not get any water at all at school.

12.   When meals are served at school, the untouchable students are made to sit separately and are served without their plates being touched.

13.   The postman throws their post from a distance.

The Vankars

There are four main scheduled castes in Gujarat:

1. The Vankars are the single largest group in the state. They were about 43 per cent of the scheduled caste population in 1961. They are known as Vankars because of their traditional occupation of weaving in some districts. They are spread over all the districts of the state except Kutch and the Dangs.

2. The second largest group numerically is formed by the Chamars. They were about 22 per cent in 1961.

3. The Bhangis form the third largest group. They were 14 per cent in 1961.

4. The Meghwals are the fourth group, being 11 per cent in 1961.

Altogether these four castes constitute about 90 per cent of the total scheduled caste population of the state.

There are nine other castes which are numerically small and about 18 more with negligible membership (Desai, 1972: 40).

The Centre's work in the Bhal has been limited almost exclusively to the Vankars. According to the 1961 census they were 585,298 or 42.81 per cent of the 1,367,255 which make up the total scheduled caste population in the state (Dushkin: 222, 187). Their relative numerical strength, together with government programmes of protective discrimination, has given them more political power than other scheduled castes have. The Minister of State for Agriculture in the Union Ministry, at the time of writing, is a Vankar from Gujarat. In the state itself, the Deputy Speaker and the Chief Party Whip are also Vankars.

Such a small minority, 2.92 per cent of the total population in Gujarat, has so much political power because of the reservation system which has given the group 11 legislators. Furthermore, most political parties have to make a show of their determination to uplift the scheduled castes. This help notwithstanding, the majority of the people, specially in the villages, are still much discriminated against.

Not all Vankars fit into a single neat category, nor do they relate to each other on a footing of equality; just the opposite. Vankars from Charotar (a geographical region within Kheda district) consider themselves superior to those in Chasi or the Bhal (two other regions within Kheda district).

Compared to those in Charotar, the Vankars in the Bhal are backward. Very few of them have attended any college, let alone the medical or engineering colleges. Although some have a few acres of land, agriculture, as we shall presently see, is not very lucrative. The majority, are either wage earners or share-croppers – the latter being by far the worst off. However, this *jati* is numerically strong in this area. In bigger villages there may be 100 Vankar households. They are despised but they cannot be ignored; low in social status, they are highly esteemed as farmhands.

Their houses, plain mud walls, a tiled roof and no windows, have one room which functions as kitchen, bedroom and living room. Few Vankars in the Bhal have pukka houses i.e. made of brick and mortar. Kerosene stoves are common, but firewood is cheaper. The smoke may fill the room, slowly finding its way out through the fissures of the mud walls and the chinks between the tiles. Such houses cannot be comfortable. Except for the cold winter nights people are more likely to spend time in the open or in a semi-covered space at the entrance where they drink tea, sleep, bathe, converse or simply while away the time when they are not out in the fields working – or answering a call of nature.

The cattle are kept close by: another threat to the hygiene of the place. All the houses, ghetto-like, are clustered together outside the village. Water must be brought from the well (a separate one for them). Electricity is slowly reaching the Bhal, but most people do not avail themselves of it, unable or unwilling to pay the small fee prescribed, although this is changing today; drainage and pavements are unwanted luxuries, even though some of the lanes are a hazard during the monsoon.

The staple food in their diet is the chapati*[1] made out of wheat flour or sometimes *bajara* and eaten with either plain chilli powder or pungent vegetables, depending on one's resources. Earlier there was an abundance of milk and home-made ghee which strengthened their diet while *chas* (buttermilk), refreshing and full of vitamins, was given freely in the fields. But the marketing genius of *Amul*, Anand's Kheda district milk cooperative, has siphoned away most of the milk in exchange for hard cash which most people are perpetually in need of. Without milk and its products, their diet has weakened considerably and the harm is already evident specially in the deteriorating health of pregnant mothers and their babies.

Poor Vankars have only the clothes they wear which they wash before they themselves bathe and wear again once dried - an easy task during summer, but an impossible one during the rains.

Malaria is the most frequent disease. Repeated attacks ravage the health of many who fail to take prophylactic care. The health authorities have been more successful in controlling cholera. Amoebic and other types of dysentery which sap the energy of many are seldom treated medically. Scabies is a scourge, being contagious and demanding hygienic measures which most can ill afford. Poor medical care turns disease into a drain on both their strength and purse.

Their economic condition is subject to the ups and downs of agriculture which is their only occupation. It is not profitable but they have no better prospects. If not a source of income, land has always been a status symbol and a means to obtain loans. The farmers' indebtedness in the Bhal, endemic and ruinous, is made easier to bear by the comforting hope of a bumper crop – ever elusive though that is. Nature is still the unpredictable lord of the Bhal, only partly subdued by human ingenuity. But things are better today. Part of the Bhal is now irrigated by the Mahi canal during the monsoon, and has been turned into lucrative paddy fields. Paddy cultivation has sharply increased and with it the demand for labourers.

---

1. * Bread made with a stiff dough of flour and water, rolled out like a pancake and baked on a grille.

During the monsoon everybody is overburdened. But being at the fag end of the canal, a niggardly monsoon may still deprive the fields of water when they need it most, thus ruining the paddy – and the people's finances.

The winter crop, usually wheat, does generate employment, but to a less extent. Thus a landless labourer is fully employed for six months and is in search of work during the rest of the year. Ironically, a year of acute drought may prove to be bountiful, government's munificence making good nature's improvidence. Relief works do provide a reasonable income without much exertion. Ordinarily, however, during the slack season people are out of work, soon enough out of cash and, ultimately driven into the hands of the moneylender.

High interest rates, a bond to work in the moneylender's field at the rates he fixes (since he needs cheaper labour during the peak season) and an agreement to have the money docked from those wages are conditions which move the most hardened usurer to dole out the needed banknotes. The borrowers lose money on the exorbitant interests as well as the wages they have to forego during the peak season because they are not free to sell their labour; indeed, the borrowers are no better than bonded labourers.

Theirs is an economic as well as social weakness: they dare not approach the Rajput moneylender themselves. Their traditional leader pleads their cause, guaranteeing both the repayment of the loan and the observance of its conditions. While he obliges his followers, he is, in turn, obliged to the moneylender who can, through him, control the Vankars. Such control, very valuable during elections, gives the Rajput access to the taluka and district power centres which strengthen further his hold on the village. The Vankars' weakness is the Rajput's strength. In a penniless community the moneylender reigns supreme.

Traditional Leadership

The traditional leaders are called *mahetars;* they perform both corporate and individual tasks. Jointly they deal with matters affecting the whole community, including the relations of the Vankars with other castes within, and matters relating to other communities outside the village. The latter are often settled in meetings of the *nat* (assembly) of all the *mahetars* of the Bhal villages. This assembly has both legislative and judicial powers over matters affecting two or more villages. It can be convoked by the leaders of one village, although they will usually consult all the big villages. The absence of any such village would invalidate the meeting; therefore, it is very important to take them into confidence. It is in such pre-convocation parleys that the place where the *nat* will meet is also decided. Cambay is chosen very often for two reasons: it is not the home turf of any *mahetar* and it gives the leaders an opportunity to visit the taluka headquarters.

Each individual *mahetar* takes care of the welfare of the households under his jurisdiction: this duty may include finding suitable partners for young boys and girls outside the village (marriages within the village are forbidden), arrangements for the marriage or subsequent divorce when the marriage fails, deciding how many people will be invited to the funeral banquet on the twelfth day after a death, arranging loans, protecting his clients when they are in trouble, etc.

A big village may have as many as ten *mahetars* and each may have jurisdiction over roughly ten households. Not every *mahetar* holds the same degree of power within the village. Personal skills and economic preponderance do give one or two of them political ascendancy in their village and in the whole region if the village is a big one. The dialectic skills of the *mahetars* are either a treat to watch or a torture to endure: cool, objective reasoning may suddenly turn into biting sarcasm, a Homeric rage into Oriental calm, a set of quick solutions may be followed by indefinite postponements. Their quick wit can annihilate a powerful opponent and, out of their unending repertoire of legends and stories, they can produce a lengthy tale to defuse a potentially explosive situation, or an unlikely one to cause deliberate confusion.

Lesser *mahetars* may even lose their rank (which is largely hereditary) or, more likely, be forced into a state of dependence on the more powerful ones – of course, the possibility of changing allegiances does give them some bargaining power.

Intercaste Relationships

Caste continues to be a significant factor in village life. What follows is not an accurate description based on the careful collection of field data; but an impressionistic picture attempting to portray the way Vankars look at other castes.

The Rajputs are the dominant caste in the Bhal where their households may be one-third cf a particular village. Most of the land is in Rajput hands, – with the richest families, that is; there are many poor families among them, too. As a community they wield both economic and political power. In the past they have succeeded in having their men elected as *sarpanches*. The local MLA is also a Rajput.

The Bharwads own less land, wield little political power and yet are a force to reckon with. Their main occupation is rearing cattle (cows and buffaloes) which often trespass into cultivated fields giving rise to quarrels. In a fight, they can be formidable as they always stand united. Their children are sent to graze the cattle, at an early age. Few of them are literate and fewer still have finished school. In a modern society this is a big handicap.

The Koli Patels were formerly a rather low caste but have moved upward in the caste hierarchy. Agriculture is their only occupation. Although not big landowners, they are politically ambitious and have already had their men elected *sarpanch* in some of the villages.

Among the lower castes the Vaghris are the most numerous. They own little land, are mostly uneducated, and, apart from agriculture, they rear goats. In villages that are close to the sea, they fish during the season. They have very little political influence and are manipulated by the higher castes. They are, however, very conscious of being *caste* people and will not mix with the Vankars.

Each caste is governed by its own caste leaders. Matters affecting various castes may be referred to either the government bureaucracy or the village *sarpanch* or, finally, to a meeting of the caste leaders concerned. Small matters are easily dealt with by the leaders of the castes involved. A village *sarpanch* can play a decisive role in such disputes if he has moral authority. Recourse to government, an outside force, is considered a loss of face for the village. Being sued in a court of law is looked upon by all, not without reason, as a misfortune. It may be the only means of self-defence in the hands of the poorer castes: it is expensive (lawyers' fees, trips to taluka headquarters, bribes, etc.) and therefore, beyond the reach of most individuals; but it can be used by the whole group.

A quarrel between members of two castes is settled not by the individuals themselves but by their leaders. This practice protects the moneylenders and political leaders who need not deal with the masses but only with their leaders. In practice a rich Rajput can easily win over the most influential Vankar leader and through him impose, say, labour conditions or settlements of individual disputes favourable to himself. In the past, this has been a common complaint raised by the Vankar rank and file against their own leaders.

When the interests of the upper caste leaders conflict, their divisions are reflected in the lower castes – some *mahetars* take sides with one, and others with other high caste leaders (not necessarily belonging to the same caste). This is one cause of factional fights, an important element which will be discussed later.

Other administrative matters, say the preparations for a village festival – what tasks will be done by which caste, what will be their contribution, etc. – are also settled by the caste leaders.

The most glaring practices of untouchability are no longer evident, but others still remain. The elders still remember those times when, if forced to approach a Rajput's house, they had to withdraw without turning, sweeping away the dust upon which they had approached so that the high castes might not be defiled by it.

Exploitation and all the social and economic injustices which go with it may easily lead to the conclusion that the perpetrators of such injustices lack any moral sense in western terms altogether or, at least that social relations are ruled by sheer arbitrariness. This is not true. Even within what may be called unjust inequality, there are clear moral rules accepted by all. Thus, for example, stealing is considered immoral.

However, if the high castes steal from the "outcastes" and the latter do not complain, this practice may with time be considered a normal one and therefore, moral. Of course, the aggrieved *jati* can always object and, with determination, can have such practices stopped. Moral indignation right at the start is a more effective and easy way to prevent unjust practices.

This point which may appear a mere academic consideration, has very important applications in activist strategy. When the scheduled castes fight against an immoral practice, accepted as such by all, the opposition of the powerful castes loses much of its sting. On the other hand, if the high castes can prove that the lower castes are unfair, unjust or immoral, then their fierceness knows no bounds. An example will clarify this point.

In one of the villages a Rajput used to have illicit relations with a Vankar woman. The Vankar men were upset by it; but, for a long time they could not take action, until during one of his forays, the Vankars were alerted. They surrounded the woman's house and commanded the Rajput to come out. His initial refusal and subsequent attempt to escape evoked violence. When he did finally come out of the house, he was hit with a spade and lay half-conscious on the ground. The Rajputs were informed; but nobody came to his rescue. They all disclaimed responsibility. Before the police arrived, he was dead. No Rajput ever raised a finger to accuse the Vankars. "He was a disgrace to our community," was their only comment.

In ordinary circumstances, the murder of a Rajput by the scheduled castes would have had dire consequences. A year and a half ago, a group of Bharwads (caste people, after all) killed a Rajput in revenge. The reaction of the Rajputs was so overwhelmingly powerful that the Bharwad menfolk fled in panic — one year later they had hardly dared to return to the village, even though a police party was posted there. Evidently, morality does play an important role in intercaste relations. Individuals do identify with their caste even if the cause is unjust (my caste right or wrong); but the way a cause is fought may vary considerably depending on how the morality of the issue is perceived.

Factional Fights

Factional fights are important for two reasons: first, they are a recurrent theme in the Vankars' conversations and a critical element in their group image. On a visit to a village, the first thing one is likely to hear of is the latest fight in the *vas* (place where they stay). When a project is discussed, the first objection to be raised will be: "We cannot do it; we cannot stand together; we are always fighting among ourselves." True to this group image, factional fights do take place; and this is the second reason why they are important. Apart from the material losses, and they can be considerable, these fights divide the Vankar *jati*, making it easy for the high caste leaders to rule over them. Indeed, upper caste leaders have a vested interest in such fights, since they are often asked to arbitrate and can thus exact their pound of flesh. They often instigate such fights and are always kept well informed of the course of events by individual Vankars eager to curry favour with them.

The worst fights are those which involve the traditional leaders. This is often the case: inveterate hostilities among the *mahetars* themselves may exist in one village. In another the increased economic or political power of one *mahetar* may rally the others to oppose his ascendancy. Indeed jealousy is commonly cited as the root cause of all fights. When two *mahetars* are at war with each other, there is no possibility of united action. One will oppose whatever the other says or does. Given the power wielded by a *mahetar*, he will carry along with himself all his followers, dividing the Vankar *jati*.

The very organisation of the Vankars (one *mahetar* for every ten households) lends itself to divisions. Five to ten leaders in one village are too large a number to sustain unity. The desire to become the acknowledged representative of the village in the region and, therefore, *the* leader within the village gives rise to power struggles which last until one of the contenders becomes the indisputable leader. The conflicting interests of each group within the village are another cause of dissension. Wounds from past quarrels may be difficult to heal.

It is only when there is no work in the *vas* that fights take place; they are set aside during the agricultural season, when everybody is busy in the fields. Although fights cause untold harm, one cannot ignore their *entertaining* role. In the Bhal there are six months during which sheer survival instinct forces people to work from dawn to dusk and beyond. Everybody works. There are other months of imposed leisure. Everybody quarrels. Being a regional pastime, quarrels must involve everybody. That is why an individual fight is quickly promoted to a factional war. A good fight keeps boredom away. Soccer, as it is played in Europe, would be a good substitute. Surely, a remedy must be found for idleness, the workshop of the devil.

At a higher level, one must accept that coexistence is not easy anywhere, that cooperation is positively difficult and that unity is, in the long run, a utopian dream.

Religion

The Vankars are predominantly Hindu, although there are a

good number of Protestants and Catholics among them, while the Muslims are very poorly represented.

Conversion to Christianity started during the last century due mainly to the efforts of Protestant pastors. Their theological approach was naively radical: everything Hindu was pagan and, therefore, had to be rooted out. In practice this meant thorough westernisation and the abolition of all those customs and practices which are the cultural heritage of any *jati*. The converts ended up by becoming a new *jati* – converted Vankars to the Hindus, but a Christian caste according to themselves. The result was a rather uncomfortable situation: the new Christians thought that conversion had turned them into a higher caste; the rest of the society thought differently.

A greater claim to upward social mobility derived from their very creditable educational performance. Not only did the Protestant pastors set up good schools and insist on sending all children to them, the more promising students were given generous scholarships to England and America. Those who returned had developed self-confidence and a cosmopolitan veneer which opened the doors to lucrative posts.

The Catholic conversion movement started much later. By then Christian theology had evolved sufficiently to detach the Christian message from western cultural expressions. Indeed, missionaries were much more respectful of the culture, the customs and traditions of the place to which they were sent. Early Catholic missionaries made a careful distinction between Hindu theology which they rejected and Hindu customs which they were ready to accept. Within the Vankar jati itself their position was often very ambivalent. But, in any case, they rejected the Protestant practice of considering the Christians a group apart which had nothing to do with the rest of the Vankars. This might have been necessitated in part by the fact that other Christian groups (mainly from Goa) already existed in Gujarat. The latter were not eager to be classed with the former.

The conversion of the Vankars in the Bhal started in earnest during the 1960s. Father Lopetegui, a Spaniard who came to Cambay at that time, affirmed that conversion to Christianity did not mean giving up social membership in one's own jati. It was only a new spiritual relationship with God through the mediation of Jesus and the visible Church on earth. As a priest his claim on his

Christians was limited to matters of faith and morals. Other social, cultural and economic matters were not his concern. His Christians had to follow the dictates of the traditional leaders like all other Vankars. Evidently, such an attitude differed sharply not only from that of the Protestants but also from that of other Catholic converts who thought that calling themselves Christian would help them change their identity. In the Bhal, Catholics called themselves Catholic Vankars. The initial movement towards Christianity was rather powerful but limited to a few individuals. The incentives given by government to Hindu scheduled castes and denied to Christians dampened the initial fervour and brought down the number of conversions considerably.

The Catholics, like the Protestants, valued education highly and made great sacrifices to have their children educated. Few could make it to the university, but many attended school. As a result, most villages in the Bhal have enough educated men to deal with the bureaucracy, set up and run cooperatives, and organise festivals with plays and songs composed and performed by themselves. However, sometimes religion becomes an issue.

Christians form their own religious *mandalis* (associations). They organise the singing at the religious ceremonies and have night-long sessions of *bhajan mandalis* when religious hymns are sung: these *mandalis* compete with the Hindu *mandalis*. Since the Christians are better educated, they have a power and influence in their own *jati* well beyond their numerical strength. This is often resented by the Hindus, leading to friction with the Christians.

It was in this world of the Bhal Vankars that the Centre began its more serious educational work.

3

THE CENTRE IN THE BHAL

The Centre's first contact with the Bhal was in May 1974. A young Rajput studying at St. Xavier's College had seen the work of the Centre in other villages and organised one of those courses described earlier for his village, which, incidentally, was not very successful. Some Vankars, a token representation chosen by the Rajputs to be able to say that they were above caste considerations, took part in the course and were the first to come into contact with the Centre. Whether through them or through other sources, the Catholic priest at Cambay came to know about the Centre and offered to send a group of Catholic Vankars for training. That was in the second half of 1974.

The same year, the first group made up exclusively of scheduled castes came to St. Xavier's College. It was not the ordinary course with participants all coming from the same caste and village. These were middle-aged men from many villages in the Bhal. They were all Christian. It was the first time, however, that the Centre moved from its educational approach based on group dynamics to that of consciousness-raising inspired by Paulo Freire, as described earlier.

Both trainers and trainees liked the course. The Centre realised that the new approach was a much more meaningful educational method. It also gained confidence that from now on it could train the scheduled castes. The participants became the best propaganda for the Centre in the Bhal. Within months two big villages, Pandad and Golana, asked to attend the Centre's courses. Table 1 lists the courses given up to 1977.

Golana was the first village to have a regular course for the majority of its Vankar households, in Ahmedabad. The result of this course was a united effort to cultivate a field owned by the Vankars. Their first attempt proved successful. But soon the old factional fights began. The enthusiastic younger leaders appealed to the Centre. A study of the situation made it clear that there was a power struggle going on between the younger and the traditional leaders.

Table 1: **Courses Given to the Bhal Villages from 1974 to 1977**

Year	Month	Village	Remarks
1974	May	Pandad	Rajputs and others
1974	October		Christians from several villages
1975	January	Golana	Vankars
1975	December	Pandad	Kharland project
1976	December	Vadgam	Vankars
1977	January	Rohini	Two small villages
		Gudel	Vankars
1977	February	Vainej	Vankars

Unity within the Vankar caste was by now topmost on the Centre's list of priorities, as a means to counteract their factional fights. Unless the traditional leaders were taken into confidence, the Centre thought, there was no possibility of united action. All these things would have to be explained to both the parties in an atmosphere of peace and tranquility.

Accordingly, a refresher course was organised in far-away Ahmedabad. Unity and leadership were its main themes. The Centre kept on asking one question of the younger leaders, "Can you fight both the Rajputs and your own leaders, your *mahetars*?" Their initial reaction was to parry the question with humour or to change the subject; but, in the end, they had to face it. And there could be but one answer. Without the cooperation of their *mahetars*, it would not be possible to fight high caste injustices. The youth came to terms with the elders; and, in the process, the possibility of united action became clearer to all. Everybody had a part to play. And the traditional leaders' role could be critical. Their administrative skills, their moral authority and power to impose discipline and to guarantee the fulfilment of conditions, their ability to rouse the whole Vankar *jati* if the occasion so demanded were too precious to be wasted. True, they could be manipulative. But manipulation could be checked if the followers were enlightened and well informed.

The second course was given to Pandad. Insistence on having this course came not only from the villagers themselves but also from Father Lopetegui in Cambay. His interest in the course was not exclusively educational.

Imaginative and far-sighted, he had acquired 578 acres of land reclaimed from the sea by government and auctioned for a song in Pandad. It was to be divided among 42 individuals later on; but government regulations demanded that those names be included in the sale deed against the plots they would eventually own. This was done by the Father, with the consent of the future owners, although no one knew exactly which plot he would finally receive. Their understanding with the Father was that the land would be cultivated jointly (the Father providing financial and technical inputs) until the loans taken to improve the land could be recovered. Thereafter each individual would take possession of his own plot.

The scheme had several flaws. First, the land was not as good as had been initially assumed. Indeed, part of the land was well beyond redemption. Except for a few good plots, most of the land would require much time and money to become economically viable. The future owners soon lost interest in the venture. Finally, there was a big question: why should those whose plots were barren be involved at all? Apart from the weaknesses of the scheme, the truancy of the owners made any joint work in these fields very difficult. Their attitude was clear: "The Fathers had invested a lot of money in the programme; it was in their interest to see that this venture succeeded. Let them take care of it."

Father Lopetegui thought that the Kharland was a good scheme - if only the people had the foresight to undergo the initial hardships which improving the land entailed. Such schemes, on the other hand, demanded much more attention and time than he could afford to give.

To begin with, he expected the Centre to educate the participants in the scheme, to see its advantages and to understand the need to implement it so that the fields could improve and start becoming productive. Later, he asked the Centre to become more actively involved, to get the project moving.

The course was given in December 1975. This, like all the courses given during these years, aimed at social awareness to make the people stand up for their rights and to fight injustice. The participants took up the challenge.

The Rajputs of Pandad had been indulging in the practice of hiding the bullock carts of the Vankars and then asking for a ransom. An ordinary individual would prefer to pay the relatively small ransom amount rather than to buy a new cart. As a result of the Centre's course they all decided to fight against this practice. They bound themselves not to pay the ransom. If the cart could not be retrieved, the whole group would pay for the new cart. Soon they had an opportunity to put their strategy to the test. A cart was stolen, word went round, mentioning the ransom figure; but instead of money, the extortioners received a summons from the court. The Vankars had filed a case. Such an unexpected reaction made the Rajputs back down. The word was now, "Withdraw the case and you get back the cart." But the Vankars wanted the matter settled once and for all. They demanded that the culprit be punished. The Rajputs preferred to fight it out in court.

The intervention of the acknowledged Rajput leader in the Bhal put an end to the case and to this unfair practice, as well. He needed the cooperation of the Vankars to fight the election of his son and was happy to help the former in order to achieve the latter. This is another instance which shows how complex intercaste relations are. True, elections do not take place every year and not all elections demand the same type of cooperation. Again, once the elections are over, life returns to its old routine. All this is true; and yet, there is no doubt that democracy has introduced a new element into caste relationships, which favours the scheduled castes.

But for all these advantages the poor Vankars had a very tough time when they asked for loans. The moneylenders made them pay dearly for their new social awareness.

Social awareness apart, the aim of the course in question was to motivate the owners of the Kharland Project to take full advantage of the newly acquired land. The matter was discussed. The participants all agreed in principle to continue the Scheme. However, a number of practical difficulties were raised. "Could the Center" the Father of Cambay then suggested, "help the Pandad people to run the Project?" It was accepted with that naive self-confidence of the inexperienced. The people in Pandad saw in this another proof that the Father's stakes in the scheme were so high that, no matter what they did, the scheme would be carried out.

The Center soon paid for its hasty decision. The Kharland Project failed to make any progress. This failure taught the Center the following lessons:

1. Before undertaking a joint venture in a village, *all* the main households of the community should be consulted.

2. If any section within that community objects to the venture, work should not be started.

3. The various sections of the community should *ask* the Centre to take up the work. The conditions governing the agreement should be well understood and *accepted* by all.

In the Kharland project, there were only 42 young men involved who represented a clearly separate section: they were mainly Christian, not Hindu; educated, they stood apart from the illiterate; younger men, they sometimes challenged the elders. When the work is accepted by the whole community, its leaders can exercise very effective control. Indeed, this experience in Pandad demonstrated the critical role which the traditional leaders could play in energising and controlling their followers. Furthermore, as we have already said, with reference to Golana, unity and joint action are impossible without the *mahetars'* cooperation.

The project had been taken over from the Fathers in Cambay. The Centre was naturally seen as a continuation of the Fathers' work. It had not been explained to the people that the Centre was neither a religious nor a charitable institution, but a professional organisation doing development work. It became very difficult to change the people's understanding *after* the Centre had started work. The only sensible option was to discontinue work and begin somewhere else. This withdrawal was also meant to convey another message: the Centre would not play games. If reasonable conditions were not accepted, it would walk out. This was a reaction to the participants of this Project who kept changing the conditions of work in the hope that, through tough bargaining, and obstructionist tactics they would obtain further benefits. Having failed to reach an understanding during the whole of 1976 and part of 1977 the Centre finally decided to withdraw from the Kharland project.

The Centre had already been working almost three years in the Bhal. Six villages had already attended its courses in Ahmedabad (Table 1). It was now time to look back and evaluate the work done so far. This was done during 1977. The results of this evaluation were disturbing. The initial impact of the courses had, no doubt, been good. New activities had been taken up, better agricultural methods were being followed, a new unity had been forged which enabled our clients to fight injustice. But when there was unemployment, when recourse to the moneylender was inevitable, then it all seemed to peter out and conditions would even look more grim. One could sense a certain despondency and even frustration among those who had attended the courses.

As far as agricultural productivity was concerned, our evaluation study showed that only those courses given to the higher castes who commanded greater resources had proved an economic success. In the case of the lower castes and poorer people, the teaching of agriculture had not led to any visible improvement in their economic situation. As experts assert, agricultural technology cannot be imparted without two other essential inputs i.e., capital investment and managerial skills or administrative knowhow.

As far as the new social awareness was concerned, the initial successes in the Vankars' fight for justice met with an alarming resistance from the moneylenders. The latter had lost some battles but, having economic power, they were confident of winning the war – a frightening possibility for the now socially aware Vankars. The Centre was shaken in its naive faith in the power of its awareness-raising exercises to transform groups of individuals who would change the course of history. Money, one almost came to think, could teach the destitute more effectively than the Centre's cleverly designed courses. The Centre's whole educational approach had to be overhauled. But first, it was necessary to study the socio-economic conditions of the Vankars more systematically. That would help to re-examine its pedagogy.

Much of 1977 was given to conducting a socio-economic survey. Table 2 sums up its findings. Indebtedness emerged as the most striking factor in this survey. When questioned as to their sources of income, the people mentioned three. Some had their own land from which, when the monsoon was sufficiently good, they received a reasonable income, while a poor monsoon meant a bad debt. That is why regular wage earners were better off than most landowners. Some persons however, could find work only during the agricultural season. The worst off were the share-croppers or those compelled to cultivate somebody else's fields at their own risk and expense and for the owner's sure benefit. Landowners, share-croppers and wage earners were unemployed for several months in the year, up to half the year. No employment meant no income, while expenditure on essentials had to be maintained. When this state of affairs was prolonged, they had no option but the moneylender, with the social and economic disadvantages this entailed. Briefly, the moneylender is ready to advance money because that is to his advantage: it ensures cheap labour for his fields. The greater the debt the stronger the bond. That is why it is called bonded labour. The life of the bonded labourer, however, is pitiful.

Table 2: Income, Expenditure and Debt of Vankars in Eight Villages (in rupees)

Village	Number Surveyed	Family Members	Expenditure	Income	Debt
Vainej	18	71	64,660	37,648	27,012
Vadgam	20	143	131,471	103,840	27,631
Pandad	21	126	102,095	73,210	28,835
Gudel	12	91	118,934	96,055	22,879
Rohini	8	63	59,702	33,579	26,123
Golana	20	111	106,647	85,609	21,038
Varasada	18	105	108,633	89,180	19,453
Galyana	19	127	101,341	63,535	37,806
	837	347	793,482	582,656	210,777

An education which did not bring about radical changes in the existing socio-economic structures was doomed to failure. By the same token, the educator who did not help to bring about such a change was not a good educator. The Centre was forced to change its tactics. What follows is the story of that change.

4

THE CENTRE WORKS
WITH THE VANKARS

From the foregoing pages the following problems appear:

1. Caste ideology has taught the Vankars to accept Rajput superiority. It has taught them that not much can be done to change the existing system of exploitation and unjust inequality.

2. Their state of indebtedness forces the Vankars to accept whatever the moneylender, the Rajput, tells them. Most of them are forced to work in his fields, on his terms. All this drives home their state of dependence on the high caste.

3. Traditional leadership is often allied to the higher castes and helps perpetuate factional fights.

4. The state of overdependence on the high caste will continue as long as the Vankars do not become economically self-sufficient.

In the light of these problems, the Centre began to draw up its priorities for work. The need to achieve economic self-sufficiency now began to attract some of the attention which had earlier been exclusively given to consciousness raising. For, without an economic basis of sustenance, the Vankars could not alter their position vis-a-vis the higher castes. Heightened consciousness alone was not enough.

To achieve economic self-sufficiency employment would have to be provided the whole year round. Ideally, of course, the best thing would be to have the whole Vankar *jati* in each village own and control the means of production. This would empower them to give employment and to distribute the surplus equitably or in the best interests of the whole *jati* group.

An enterprise owned and controlled by the whole community would make unity, self-respect and cooperation an experienced reality. Whatever had been accepted in the courses could be put into practice and, therefore, powerfully internalised in daily work experience.

The goal was beautiful; but its implementation would not be easy. As the idea was first mooted in small groups of younger Vankars, the following difficulties were mentioned:

1. The *mahetars* would prove the most serious obstacle. Without their agreement and active help no serious venture could be taken up. On the other hand, past experience had proved that their involvement usually led to manipulation or the use of the enterprise for their selfish ends.

2. Those who had land would first take care of their own fields, often ignoring community work. What was worse, most people would look on any common venture as a means to enrich themselves at the expense of the community.

The first difficulty had already been a matter of much reflection within the Centre. The *mahetars* had to be involved; therefore powerful checks had to be built into the establishment and running of any enterprise, to prevent manipulation. Conceptually, the cooperative had to be based on a contract, proceeding from sheer economic interest rather than from complex affective states, habits, and traditions. Otherwise the *mahetars* would reign supreme, traditional beliefs would hold sway, even factional fights might rage furiously.

This would demand the active involvement of all. The interest of all must check the dysfunctionality of some. The power of tradition and the *sacral*, bordering on the magical, must be balanced by the *rational* and *secular* activity of an economic enterprise.

The second difficulty i.e. the possibility of mismanagement or, at worst, legal absconding, frightened the Centre. State regulations did not allow an individual or trust which did not belong to the scheduled castes to be a member of a scheduled caste cooperative. The Centre risked making loans which clever individuals might easily appropriate to themselves. What if the executive committee refused to return the loan or, worse still, kept all the money of the cooperative for the committee members themselves.

An enlightened and helpful government official showed us a way out.

Call the Registrar of Cooperatives to the general body meeting and have them all pass a resolution to appoint one of your men as paid secretary of the cooperative with the power to sign cheques. The cooperative cannot have this man removed from office without the Registrar's permission. This will take care of your difficulties for some time, at least. The long range viability of the cooperative will depend on your educational efforts.

With these two problems solved, the Centre was ready to launch its own cooperative movement. It would insist on the following conditions:

1. All the households of the Vankars in a given village should belong to the cooperative.

2. The Centre would take on a cooperative *only* after *all* the households had bought their corresponding part in the shares of the cooperative.

3. All the assets should be owned by the cooperative. In other words, the cooperative would refuse to take up any work in fields belonging to individuals.

4. The Centre would advance money to the cooperative on the understanding that if the enterprise succeeded, all the money advanced to the cooperative would have to be returned to the Centre for similar work in other villages; on the other hand, if the economic venture failed, the Vankar *jati* would have no obligation to return the money.

5. The executive committee of the cooperative should be elected by *all* the members of the cooperative who would also have the right to examine the accounts and to receive all pertinent information regarding the administration of the cooperative .

The proposed cooperative movement would make fresh demands on the Centre. Technical personnel would be needed. The Centre had always viewed with suspicion the idea of running development projects. Villagers attending the Centre's courses had time and again complained about the projects being run in their villages. From their explanations it was clear that they all looked at those projects as a cheap means of acquiring something. Development and high ideals like justice, equality, unity and cooperation lost much of their meaning, once a project was under way. When any outside agency insisted on such ideals, the people were irritated and inclined to suspect the outsider's goodwill. On closer scrutiny, it was found out that those running projects were often more concerned with material accomplishments than with their clients' understanding and acceptance of the project. There was a logic in such behaviour. Money had been received from funding agencies to carry out a well-defined plan (else, no agency would give a grant); sometimes an initial agreement had been reached by the people concerned and then when a considerable amount of money had already been spent, some people would raise doubts. How could the project holder stop midstream? And if the people refused to go along, how could the money already spent be justified? It was so much easier to use pressure tactics to *persuade* the people who, most of the time, would play along. The Centre itself had been the victim of such games in the Kharland project.

To ward off this danger, the Centre decided to set up two wings: one educational and one technical. The former would have the power to override any decision taken by the latter, when the good of the villagers or their legitimate interests demanded it. In so doing, the Centre, unwittingly, transferred the inevitable friction in running a project from the village to the Centre itself.

By the end of 1977, having decided to change its educational approach, the Centre made several feasibility studies to find out how best to start a cooperative. A loan scheme to purchase buffaloes was studied first. Milk producers' cooperatives had proved successful in some tribal areas. The study showed that such a scheme would not be viable in the Bhal, because of the scarcity of fodder. An earlier plan to start a credit system was given up as soon as the results of the socio-economic survey, mentioned earlier, came into our hands. Banks in the region had outstanding loans to the tune of Rs. 2,400,000.

A third plan to set up a service cooperative which would help farmers improve their productivity and obtain higher prices for their produce was also studied. Again the results of our socio-economic survey showed that most agricultural crops were a net loss if the labour of the owners was counted as an expense – with the exception of paddy in irrigated areas. People would not be able to pay for the services of the cooperative.

Land was easily available in many villages but it was of poor quality. Government had very generously given large tracts of land to the scheduled castes (government was not slow to advertise such progressive policy); but nothing grew in these barren fields. Two villages, Galiana and Golana, however, did have fertile fields owned by the Vankars. That would make a good start.

The Centre first went to Galiana, the plan was explained in meetings of all interested people. Ratna Dana was the undisputed leader of Galiana and one of the cleverest *mahetars* in the Bhal. He was quick to grasp all the implications of the cooperative as proposed by the Centre. His word was law in the village and he saw no reason why a new dispensation should be granted to his subjects. The Centre's conditions were not accepted. It moved out of Galiana.

Golana came tantalisingly close to accepting the cooperative – but for the scheming of one of the *mahetars*, a stooge of the Rajputs. The legendary figure of Gaga Natha, on the decline but powerful still, had not yet seen the advantages to his community and, ultimately, to himself, which the Centre's offer provided. The Golana plan had to be given up, as well.

Smarting under the pain of its failure both in the Kharland project and in its earlier educational approach – the educator comfortably removed from economic and managerial tasks –; and full of uncertainties and doubts about its new financial, technical and managerial role, the Centre now faced opposition to its new plan from the biggest villages in the Bhal: Pandad, Galiana and Golana. The future looked very bleak indeed.

Vadgam was another village which had attended a course in Ahmedabad. It had a sizeable Vankar population, 68 households. But they were divided into three factions with two redoubtable leaders always at war with each other. Government had given them 180 acres of land on lease; but it had not been put to productive use. To obtain the land a group of Vankars representing the whole *jati* had set up a cooperative. That was an advantage. But government threatened to take away the land since it had not been cultivated. Dire need prompted Vadgam to accept the Centre's plan for the cooperative. The people would see to it that all households belonged to the cooperative, that all the members of the executive were democratically elected. . . All the conditions were accepted.

The Centre accepted the opportunity. A committee was quickly formed and unity apparently achieved in a village where three factions were at each other's throats. But this proved to be not a miracle but a contrivance. By the time the Centre finally moved in to start operations, two Vankars lay in hospital, victims of the latest outburst.

"That's normal," the Centre's staff were told in almost biblical terms. "There is a time to quarrel and a time to work together." And they were as good as their word - the cycle of quarrels and cooperation succeeded each other with amazing regularity.

When the Centre offered the services of one of its men as paid secretary to the cooperative, the suggestion was gratefully accepted by the leaders who now felt themselves free from the onerous responsibility of deciding which faction would control the purse. The three factions were well represented in the committee and, this time at least, they found it easy to elect a chairman acceptable to all.

True to its commitment to the will of the people, the Centre accepted the suggestion of the committee to start agricultural operations straightaway. The result was a failure, galling to the Centre, but a dubious consolation to the elders happy at the discomfiture of the urbanites.

In those inhospitable wastes the only visible sign of life is the mesquite (*Prosopis juliflora*) − timid, shrivelled, languishing for lack of water. In the flat plains of the Bhal, roads must be raised to avoid flooding during the monsoon, by digging out the earth from the two sides and thus forming two trenches all the way. The water collects there and with water the mesquite grows profuse and exuberant adorning the landscape with its dark green foliage. It provides cheap fuel to the needy but provident farmers.

Available literature on agriculture in semi-arid zones prescribes the *Prosopis juliflora* to combat the desert, to reclaim saline lands and also to run a commercial plantation since its wood can be sold as fuel. Excellent charcoal can also be prepared from it. Its pods, high in proteins, can be used as animal feed. Evidently, on poor unirrigated land, agriculture was not economically viable, all the more so in the case of a cooperative which had to pay daily wages. Afforestation making use of the mesquite would both improve the land and earn much-needed hard cash.

A proposal to start a mesquite plantation was submitted to the Vadgam cooperative's executive committee. It was received with consternation, dismay and utter disbelief. "We shall become," one of them said, "the laughing-stock of the village. Imagine our cooperative growing the *mad bawal!*" That is the name given to this plant locally, a pointer to the low esteem in which it is held.

The reaction of the committee showed that the time was not yet ripe. A few months and several agricultural failures later, the secretary broached the matter once more to the executive committee from an entirely different angle. "Please, answer the following questions. First, 'does anybody have leisure during the peak agricultural season?' If not, then, second, 'why do you want the cooperative to go in for agriculture which will increase your work when you are already overburdened? Why don't you take up forestry which will give you work when you are unemployed?'"

The implication was clear: forestry alone made sense. Questions of prestige, the inability to figure out how such a despised shrub could yield any income, the dead weight of the past, made it difficult for the people to accept the new proposal. When they did finally agree they did it reluctantly, putting all the responsibility on the Centre. "The permission is ours, the work is yours," they said.

During the monsoon of 1979 the first nursery was set up to provide 70,000 saplings of a plant, *Prosopis juliflora* to the botanists, mesquite to the Americans and *mad bawal* to the local population. The involvement of the people was as low as the excitement of the Centre was high. It was the price of innovation. "Let them see and they will change," the Centre hoped. For the time being, however, the old professors themselves had to take up the work of transplantation — one drove the tanker, the other directed a brigade of hired hands to dig out the pits at the exact geometrical distance and the only expert took care of directing the women in the delicate task of slitting the plastic bags and depositing the muddy saplings in the pit. About 70 acres were thus transplanted in a mighty effort which showed very poor results. Only 35 per cent of the plants survived. It wasn't much; but it was the beginning. The Centre has never looked back since. While some of the plots were a total failure, in others the survival rate was high.

Subsequent care and gap filling soon made some of the plots look promising – row after row of geometrically aligned plants. "There was method," the Vadgam Vankars could not but think, "in this *mad bawal* plantation." What abstract reasoning could not do, the actual sight of the field did accomplish. Involvement was no longer a problem. The Centre's first cooperative was already in existence. And when, four years later, commercial production started everybody had to reckon with a new reality. By that time the Centre had also refined its own ideas on the cooperative movement it wanted to spearhead.

The Cooperative*[1]

Ever since Robert Owen (1771-1856) and Dr. William King (1786-1865) inspired the Rochdale Pioneers, a consumers' movement in England and Charles Fourier (1772-1837), Louis Blanc (1811-1882), Phillippe Buchez (1796-1865) and more recently, Charles Gide (1847-1932) promoted in France the idea of productive societies, cooperativism has become a familiar concept all over the world.

The agricultural cooperative movement, this paper's main concern, originated in Germany

where Friederich Wilhelm Raiffeisen (1818-1888) and Wilhelm Haas (1839-1913) built up within a few years a fairly complete system of rural cooperation, including credit, supply and later, marketing. Similar efforts were made by Luigi Luzzati (1841-1927) in Italy and Abbe de Lemmerais (1782-1854) in France in the field of agricultural cooperative credit and at a later stage by Sir Horace Plunkett (1854-1932) in Ireland in the field of cooperative dairy industry. (Helm, 1968: 2)

The modern cooperative movement was formally introduced in India in 1904 with the promulgation of the Indian Cooperative Societies Act. To a considerable extent the Act was the outcome of deliberations among government officials and leaders of public opinion who were interested in protecting peasant cultivators

----
1. * The rest of this chapter has already been published, in modified form in our *Annual Report*, 1985-87.

from the exploitative activities of money-lenders-cum-traders. In the beginning, cooperatives confined their activities to providing cheap credit to farmers. Gradually, and particularly after Independence, cooperative activity was extended to other spheres such as banking, marketing and processing. Cooperation soon became one of the instruments of rural development. Successive Five Year Plans have emphasised the importance of cooperation in the field of agricultural development and assigned an important role to cooperatives for implementing development programmes in rural areas (Baviskar, 1980: 2).

Concrete material needs or ideology may give rise to a cooperative. First there are those cooperatives which are established to answer a very concrete need. Thus, for example, several people may realise that they could buy the same commodities at a reduced price if they set up a cooperative store. As a result consumer societies may come into existence. Or several persons in need of housing may form a cooperative housing society in order to have a home at a price they can afford. This is the most common understanding of cooperativism.

Most people think of cooperatives as organisations of farmers, fishermen and the like in marketing units; of workers in labour unions; of professional groups in professional associations, and of small businessmen in cooperative wholesale purchasing. They are voluntary groups who have realised the necessity to protect themselves from vested interests: farmers organised in more than a dozen kinds of marketing cooperatives, around a particular product, such as milk, grain, livestock, fruit, cotton, etc., which have developed from local to regional to national associations; workers organised into both craft and industrial unions which are local, national and international; organisations of small businessmen who, confronted by the danger of ruin from the competition of corporate chains, have organised their own cooperative wholesales to meet such competition (Bowen, 1953: 54).

The cooperatives in the Bhal have not developed from within; but, we may say, have been imposed from without. The reason is that the people are very skeptical about cooperatives. In the experience of these people, a cooperative (or *mandali*, as they call it), usually serves the interests of particular clever individuals who contrive to siphon off aid given to the cooperative by outside agencies including government. Such individuals, for their part, generally see a cooperative as a money-making venture for themselves. Small wonder that the Vankars in the Bhal showed little enthusiasm. Significantly, they never spoke of the cooperative (*sahakari mandali*) but of the organisation (*sanstha*) of Ahmedabad. That *sanstha* meant something: money, influence, power − unlike the *sahakari mandali* which nobody would trust.

There is a great variety of cooperatives in India, consumers', housing, milk producers', agricultural, forest labourers', credit, multipurpose, etc. "In the field of cooperation," Baviskar laments, "there are many more stories of failure than of success . . ." (1980: 3-4). And then he goes on to analyse the reasons:

Where cooperatives are imposed from above by the government or similar authority as a part of development/welfare programmes they fail to enlist the enthusiasm and active participation of their members . . .

Member-controlled cooperatives are generally managed by leaders elected by their shareholders. There is no easy formula to ensure the emergence of honest and efficient leaders. . .Most cooperatives founder on the rock of corruption. The temptation to profit at the cost of the organisation appears to be too powerful for leaders to resist easily.

The farmers of the Bhal fit the norm.

Although the Vankars resisted the idea of the cooperative because of their negative experiences with the cooperatives around, the Centre insisted on cooperativism for both practical and ideological reasons. The cooperative was a convenient tool for helping *all* households; it was accepted by the law which allows special cooperatives for the scheduled castes; government offered special help like land and finances to people who organised themselves into cooperatives.

But there were also ideological considerations. In this the Centre followed recent developments in cooperativism, the producers' cooperatives. E.S. Greenberg (1986: 15-23) mentions these ideological trends:

1. *The Transcendence of Alienation* . . . Alienation whether understood as an objective situation of powerlessness and thwarted human creativity or as any of a series of subjective psychological adjuncts to that situation, adheres to a set of social relations in which workers are divorced from the control of the production process, the use of their own labour power, and the fruits of their labour. The transcendence of alienation, it follows, is possible, in the socialist tradition, only in a situation in which worker subordination is displaced by worker *superordination*. In the call for such a transformation one may locate an important source of the persistent socialist fascination with workplace democracy and worker self-management.

2. *Participatory democracy*. Participation . . . is not confined to what we normally think of as politics, but must encompass the entire society. . .participation is the principal social process by which human beings, practising the arts of self-direction, cooperation, and responsibility, liberate their capacities and thereby become whole, healthy and integrated persons. As a consequence of participation, the individual develops the attitudes and skills essential to participation in other social spheres including the political. Participation in decision making at the workplace is thus central to the democratic vision and basic to the good society.

3. *The transcendence of capitalism*. The third great tradition . . . is that which rejects both the anarchy and injustice of market capitalism and the tyranny of Soviet-style socialism in favour of "socialism with a human face" —self-governing socialism . . . Theorists in this tradition, for obvious reasons, have concluded that Marxist-Leninist vanguard methods inevitably pervert the ultimate goals of socialism (Horvat, 1982). They also argue that because of their de-emphasis on popular participation, the parliamentary, electoral strategies of Social Democracy are both ineffective for the construction of a socialist society and destructive of the ultimate values and goals of self-governing socialism. Out of this twin rejection . . . has emerged a search for a new strategy of social change in which workplace democracy, particularly in its most highly developed form — worker self-management – plays a pre-eminent role.

These trends have assumed a different shape in the Centre's understanding of cooperativism because of local circumstances.

The Cooperative Movement's Ideology

The main goal of this movement in the Bhal is to bring about a radical change. The Vankars are enslaved in a set of oppressive social relations because of both the caste system itself and their economic situation – each reinforcing the other. They are either marginal or landless farmers who depend entirely on the upper caste landowners. Agricultural labour being seasonal, they remain unemployed for several months. Without any income and without savings from the previous season, most of them fall inevitably into the hands of the upper caste moneylender thus further strengthening both their economic subjugation and the prevailing discriminatory caste relations. The dominant caste leaders have managed to divide the lower castes thus depriving them of any power to organise themselves and fight for their rights.

The Centre in these circumstances has very definite goals: to achieve unity, to restore self-respect and to develop the cooperative and organisational power of these people. These goals demand radical changes in the socio-economic structures.

The Centre has understood radical change not as the abolition of private property even among the would-be cooperators; but as the setting up of new units of production which are owned and controlled by the whole community. This common ownership is meant to complement the meagre individual means of subsistence which may sometimes accrue from privately owned land. It is, therefore, a "mixed economy" at the micro level, just as there is a mixed economy at the national level.

Radical change, more specifically, is taken to mean (1) technological change or a transformation of the productive forces, raising the level of land and labour productivity through new farming methods in hitherto unproductive wastelands thus providing employment and an increased income; and (2) a more just set of social relations in which unity, cooperation and self-respect become possible. This implies (a) ownership and control of the means of production, (b) an administrative and organisational set-up open to, and controlled by, all and (c) an ideology which stresses justice and equality, unity and cooperation within a new vision of society which makes sense to the cooperators. The above is a tall order which demands closer scrutiny.

Technological change. Technology is here taken to mean the available set of specific techniques through which inputs are transformed into outputs: inputs like nature and human labour into outputs like commodities, machines or instruments of production (non-human capital) and better fed, housed, educated and skilled human beings (human capital). Relevant technological changes are made to achieve higher productivity. This often means the transfer of a better technology available somewhere else or upgrading one's own technology. Real *transfer of technology* takes place when all the people involved assimilate that technology, viz. when they understand it and see why it should be applied in their enterprise. When poor people set up a new enterprise they may either have an inefficient production process because of its obsolete technology but which the people fully know and understand; or they may have a technologically advanced enterprise which can compete with the rest of the country but which is run by outsiders in possession of a new brahminical knowledge. Neither possibility makes for radical change in the existing techno-material conditions; the first because it falls short of the productivity it could achieve and the second because it continues to keep the poor dependent on others. Neither, therefore, can give rise to new and more meaningful social relations.

Table 3. **Changes Sought through the Cooperative**

WHERE	HOW	WHY
Productive forces	Technological change	Higher productivity, higher income, more employment.
Social relations		To achieve
ownership and		justice, equality,
control	New administrative and	self-respect
democratic	managerial set-up	
set-up	Educational inputs	
a new ideology		

In this fast-changing and technically advancing world, power lies ultimately with those who can best harness science to their local needs. Gone are the days when one could dream of an isolated local autonomous life. Knowledge is power. Either the people avail themselves of the existing knowledge and place themselves on a footing of equality with those who know or else they accept a subordinate place – and allow themselves to be ruled by others. Any enterprise which does not keep upgrading itself is bound, sooner or later, to succumb to the cruel dynamics of a business enterprise. The importance of technological upgrading and innovation is detailed in the next chapter.

Effective transfer of technology is not easy. It presupposes a knowledge of the people concerned, their social, economic, religious background, their cultural and educational level, their scientific and technical attitudes and skills. Knowledge is also required both of the local resources and of the available technology - the latter being a very demanding task indeed in this expanding world of science and technology.

Technology plays a twofold role in development. First, it ensures the competitiveness of the new enterprise and, second, it raises the awareness of the cooperators. This last point deserves some explanation.

Technology is applied science. An effective transfer of technology presupposes that people understand it and all the scientific principles therein involved. As people imbibe more and more science, they move away from that magical or naive consciousness to a critical one. This new understanding renders impossible any return to their former slavish acceptance of others. Indeed, it is an accepted fact that technological development plays an important role in shaping the social structure of a particular group.

Ownership of the means of production. In an agricultural setting the means of production is mainly land, though water and other resources also play an important part. Ownership here means that all the members of this scheduled caste group jointly own the land. Ownership means one thing in a capitalist world of private property and something quite different when many people own the same thing – in this case, land. In the former case there is a sense of possessiveness arising from the exclusive use of property which confers the right not only to its usufruct but also to its alienation by selling or bequeathing it; while in the latter case there is a sense of shared wealth and common control to have the usufruct equitably distributed. To those to whom ownership means possessiveness, shared wealth makes little sense. Such people are likely to look at the cooperative as something "to draw advantage from," and not as something which is theirs.

This is the danger whenever the cooperative does not arise from within but is imposed from outside – as it was in our case. This danger can be avoided if the cooperative does satisfy an important need of each cooperator and makes people aware that community problems can be solved through joint action. This realisation builds up the people's faith in the cooperative movement, and helps the cooperators to move from the idea of ownership as possessiveness to the idea of common ownership or shared wealth. This understanding alone will make the cooperative socially viable over a period of time. An important way of achieving this transition is to make sure that ownership also means effective control.

Control of the means of production. The main purpose of common ownership is precisely to control the means of production so that the advantages – and the responsibilities – are equally shared by all. When ownership and therefore control is in the hands of one person alone he can do as he likes. However, when several people exercise that control the danger of conflicting interests arises, and so does the temptation to seek power within the organisation to further one's own selfish interests. *Shared* wealth both confers rights and imposes duties. If each one has the right to an equal share in the benefits, so does he have the duty to be alert and vigilant to prevent unfair practices. The benefits accruing to each cooperator will vary as the enterprise grows. Thus, in the early stages, the cooperative may only be able to provide employment during the slack season: later on, however, the enterprise may make a profit. In either case individuals control the cooperative to make sure that either the available labour and just wages or the financial benefits are justly distributed among all the households.

There is another meaning of control which is much more technical and of greater relevance to the economic health of the organisation: control over the policy followed either in the production process, in marketing or in the financing pattern itself. All this has to do with the management of the enterprise.

Management plays a critical role in any enterprise. Decision-making and implementation are the twin tasks of management. Efficient implementation demands administrative skills at both the office level (accounts, correspondence, etc.) and in the field handling the work force and making sure that the planned activity is carried out properly.

Decision-making embraces all the aspects of the enterprise, i.e. production, marketing, finances and personnel. It involves first planning and later the monitoring and evaluation of the plan's performance, thus preparing the ground for subsequent plans.

Our target group's traditional leadership can handle human problems like the marshalling of a work force, the resolution of conflicts, the disciplining of errant members. It can also take care of conventional agriculture on ordinary farms. But it is ill-equipped to effect changes from one system of production to another (say from agriculture to forestry) or to manage large tracts of land demanding sizeable mobilisation of resources and creating complex logistical problems over and above the difficulty of keeping accounts in a manner acceptable to government. Therefore, control of the means of production means the preparation of managerial cadres from among the cooperators who can run the cooperative honestly and competently.

Theoretically, the cooperators can hire managers and still own and control the enterprise — just as big industrial houses do. Psychologically, however, it makes a big difference whether outsiders or the cooperators themselves manage the cooperative. Self-management gives rise to a feeling of legitimate pride which affects the morale of the whole community. Those sections of society which have been exploited for centuries inherit diffidence, the root cause of their overdependence. In such cases development means banishing diffidence and restoring self-confidence. Therefore, it is very important to hand over as many managerial tasks to the cooperators as possiblle.

Summing up: control over the means of production gives rise to two different problems. The first is how much administrative and managerial power is the Centre wielding at present and how much can be handed over in the future. In other words, is the Centre preparing a managerial cadre of cooperators imbued with the right values and equipped with the necessary skills? The answer to this question is linked to the plan to set up a federation which will take up the managerial tasks performed at present, by the Centre. Evidently, an individual cooperative cannot prepare managers who can prepare a long-term or even a short-term plan in the areas of finance, production or marketing. On the other hand, the Federation can gradually achieve this goal — even though it might require outside expert assistance.

The second question is, what kind of control can all the cooperators exercise over the enterprise?

Table 4. Various Types of Control over the Enterprise

Policy:	Production	Finance	Marketing	Distribution
Short term	D	D	N	D
Long term	I	N	N	D

Type of Control: D = Direct; I = Indirect; N = No Control.

The present enterprise is a social forestry cooperative. Given the magnitude of the task – about 1,500 acres in the whole area – the enterprise does raise planning, logistical and marketing problems which require new skills. But on the whole the present enterprise is not so sophisticated and the managerial problems are not so involved that they cannot be explained to, and understood by the local population over a period of time, provided, of course, the right pedagogy is followed. Evidently, the same yardstick cannot be applied to industries in which the complexity of production (or marketing and financing for that matter) demands specialised skills. In such cases, even internationally acclaimed cooperatives (like Mondragon) do not pretend to give their cooperators control over the financing pattern, the production system or the marketing strategy. Theirs is only control over the distribution of benefits.

How much control can the cooperators in a social forestry cooperative have? In Table 4 the various possibilities are shown. The minimum required is that the cooperators control, directly or indirectly, the distribution of benefits. On the other hand, it is not realistic to expect all cooperators to control long-term policy as regards financing or marketing – although any effort in that direction (given the relative simplicity of the present cooperatives) would greatly help their success. How this can be done would require further study which, given the actual problems of the cooperative, is not a priority.

If direct control over most of the managerial tasks of the cooperative is not possible, an indirect form can be achieved if its power structures remain democratic. The state laws make provisions for elections to the executive committee and for the selection of a outside expert assistance.

chairman. However, these provisions are not sufficient to ensure a democratic process. Here and everywhere else "eternal vigilance is the price of freedom." All cooperators must remain alert to what is happening in the cooperative, to check possible manipulators. While ordinary members are usually extremely eager to see that wages and grain are justly distributed, the same cannot be said of short and long-term decisions taken by the cooperative. Here alertness presupposes knowledge of the implications of such decisions. Therefore, democracy demands education. Here as with the transfer of technology it is only when everybody knows that self-management becomes a possibility.

A new ideology. Ownership and control of the means of production, transfer of technology, new administrative and managerial skills, a democratic set-up, all these are but expressions of a desire; to use the cooperative as a tool for radical change, a new socio-economic structure which turns former wage-earners into owners, former beggars into legal title-holders, former dependents on the Rajputs into autonomous economic entities. The aim is to have the cooperative incarnate a movement into a visible and concrete organisation. Two elements, therefore, must be clearly distinguished: the *inner element*, call it spirit, culture, ethos, values, which cannot be immediately perceived and the *external*, clearly discernible, *structure*. When an organisation is part of accepted culture, its inner element is not terribly important; but should it run counter to prevalent values, the inner element becomes critical – an important point which requires some elaboration.

A new structure requires a new understanding, else people will look at the cooperative not as their enterprise but as another form of dependence, better perhaps because the Rajput is replaced by the more distant and easier-to-handle urbanite. Relations within the cooperative will be based on *manipulation*: the local population trying to outsmart the outsiders and each individual all the others. The new supervisor may be eager to take the place of the high caste persons whom he secretly admires because he has internalised their values; in such cases he is likely to treat his brethren much more harshly than the Rajputs did. The cooperative may become a new battleground where the traditional leaders fight each other, often reflecting upper caste rivalries. Nothing has changed.

A new spirit is required; a new understanding of society and, more specifically, of the caste system, whereby each individual is a

worthy person who has inalienable rights regardless of his or her
position in the caste hierarchy and whose inner qualities are more
important than his or her circumstances like power, wealth, sex or
birth. This understanding of society gives rise to a new self-image in
which self-respect and legitimate pride in oneself and one's own
community replaces the inferior-superior polarity; where unity and
cooperation leading to action replace fatalism and a slavish attitude
towards the forces militating against the poor. This was the new
ideology, first discussed during the courses and subsequently in the
villages themselves; it found expression in the cooperative.
Gregariousness has given way to a new organisational ability which
has energised the whole community into constructive action.

How Far Has This Movement Been Successful?

Technological change. A new technology has been introduced.
Proof of it is that more than 162 hectares of wasteland have now
become productive, that in an additional 139 work is in progress and
that as a result of this work about 500 households spread over nine
villages have found employment during the slack season (see next
chapter for a more detailed exposition). However, this is but the
beginning of a process. It is necessary to diversify and to introduce
further technological changes which may consolidate and strengthen
the present gains.

A new set of social relations. The new social relations may refer
either to other groups (more specifically higher castes) or to the
relations within the lower caste itself. To the extent to which the
ownership and control of the cooperative has become operational a
more just set of social relations should come into existence. We take
each point separately.

Common ownership. In four villages the cooperatives legally own
all the land, while in two villages, although the former owners have
in practice transferred the land to the cooperative, the legal deed has
not yet been finalised due to a legal technicality. Three villages have
no property. They run nurseries for the other cooperatives. In the
nine villages all the Vankar households have equal shares in the
cooperatives. Having their own cooperative, working in their own
fields − or at least, not in the fields of the higher castes − having
work the whole year round and receiving just wages, all these things
have dramatically lessened their economic and psychological

dependence on, and increased their bargaining power with, the upper castes.

However, have the cooperators moved from the spirit of possessiveness to the idea of shared wealth? Do they, consequently, look at the cooperative as *their* enterprise, rather than a useful contrivance for employment during the slack season? Do they have a new sense of legitimate pride in the achievements of the cooperative as their achievement or do they look at it as the work of an urbanite agency? Have they, as a result of that pride, formed a new community, strengthened their mutual bonds of unity and cooperation and thereby have their social relations within their own community improved?

It is difficult to give an answer to these questions at this moment. And yet there are areas where progress is evident: our Centre's involvement in the administration and management of the cooperatives has decreased dramatically. The accounts, the supervision, the implementation of plans, the preparation of budgets, most of the work with the bureaucracy – all this is done by officers chosen from among the local cooperators. As the local cooperators take over from the outside agency the credibility of the cooperative as *their* enterprise increases. On the other hand, the efficiency, competence and honesty with which the work in the cooperatives is carried out have earned them a high reputation both within their own community of Vankars and with other communities. This success of the cooperatives makes it easier for the cooperators to identify with the movement. Again, the fact that each individual does receive tangible benefits from the cooperative, and the fact that each individual can check the way these benefits are distributed, makes them both alert and involved. In short, the process of identifying with the cooperative and of taking pride in it as their own enterprise is in progress. On the negative side, the poorer cooperators, those who are weaker within their own community, while benefiting economically from the cooperative do not have enough knowledge and understanding of it. These people may easily be manipulated by discontented persons who have failed to join the upper cadres in the movement – precisely because the cooperative is a success, the posts of managers and accountants are coveted power centres. If much has been accomplished at the top, much still remains to be done with the rank and file.

Control of the means of production. As mentioned earlier, control raises two questions: First, how far does the outside agency transfer its power to the local cooperators and, second, how far do individual cooperators control the enterprise.

The first question has been partly answered. The local cooperators have taken over the ordinary administration which includes accounts and implementation of approved plans. The Centre still handles the decision of short and long-term policy as regards finance, marketing and production. However, the short-term production policy is, to a very large extent, already being decided by the local managers. Within one year the cooperatives will form a federation where outside agencies like the Centre, according to present legislation, can wield no power. The Centre's expectation is that by then all the short-term policies will be handled by the local people. Long-term policy will require expert guidance for some time. This, however, can be given on a consultancy basis: the Centre plans to join the federation in the only capacity allowed by the law, as a well-wisher – a second class membership without any voting rights.

As for the second question (how far do individuals control the cooperative): First, the cooperators do exercise direct control over the distribution of benefits, in the present circumstances. As of today, the only real benefit of the cooperative is the supply of employment and wages during the slack season. A system has been devised whereby all households have equal access to the cooperative's employment opportunities. There is no doubt that all the cooperators control the cooperative in the distribution of work and wages. Any real or apparent unfair practice is loudly contested by the aggrieved party. This attitude forces both the supervisors and the managers to remain alert: a proven malpractice means instant dismissal.

This does not answer a future question: what about the distribution of benefits when the cooperative makes a profit? Since no cooperative is making a profit at present, this question has not been discussed sufficiently by the cooperators. And yet the future of the cooperative will be decided when it becomes a real economic power. The stakes then will be high. The temptation to manipulate the cooperative structure for selfish purposes may prove irresistible. If the majority of its members remain vigilant, the clever few can be checked and the cooperative will remain at the service of all. Otherwise, these cooperatives will also go "the way of all flesh."

Decisions regarding short and long-term policy about finance and marketing are likely to be taken by the federation and therefore individual cooperators may have only indirect control—through the representatives they elect to the federation. Short-term production policy, on the other hand, can be controlled by individual cooperators, provided a greater effort is made to explain it to them. True, at present, plans prepared by the managers are explained to, discussed and finally approved, rejected or modified by, the committee. But a large number of ordinary members do not evince sufficient interest and to that extent their involvement is not satisfactory. Something similar can be said about short-term financial policy.

Of more immediate concern to the main leaders in all the villages is appointment to the various posts within the federation. (Those within the cooperative are decided within the village.) So far, these appointments have been made by the Centre strictly on merit. Much time and energy have been spent in training those officers. Evidently, they wield much power already and later on when the Centre's controlling influence disappears their power is bound to increase. Therefore, factions vie with one another, as do villages, to have their own men in the federation's key posts.

This problem must be viewed against the leadership pattern still prevailing among the Vankars in the Bhal. Traditional leaders still possess too much power. They can easily use the cooperative to further their narrow factional interests. In the past, appointments within the cooperative itself were used to bring factional fights into the cooperative. Thus, for example, each cooperative has one supervisor who necessarily belongs to one of the factions. The leader of the opposite party can easily rally round all his followers with the war cry, "our side must have a supervisor," turning the cooperative into a factional battleground. Such fights have paralysed one of the cooperatives for several months. So far, however, the rank and file's dire need of work has eventually forced the leaders to come to an understanding. In another village the cooperative was totally derailed as one of the factions set up its own cooperative excluding the other faction altogether. On the other hand, the other eight cooperatives have been able to deal with this problem effectively.

A democratic set-up. Too much power in the hands of the traditional leaders does definitely militate against the democratic principle. Indeed one wonders to what extent there are democratic elections within the cooperative and to what extent the whole thing is a process used by the traditional leaders to make their own choices. As long as the latter remains a possibility, the interests of the poorer households are likely to be ignored. On the other hand, the educational work done within the village has brought about qualitative changes in the common man's understanding of his rights. When fear of the upper caste subsides, the courage to challenge one's own leaders increases.

The democratic structures do exist: First, *all* the households of the scheduled caste belong to the cooperative. Given the contempt in which the latter are held by the caste people, a cooperative open to all castes would in practice mean an organisation run by the high castes. Meaningful political involvement of the former untouchables presupposes a degree of economic self-sufficiency and social acceptance which at present does not exist. The Centre insists on unity and understands that unity in a restricted sense, that is, the unity of the untouchables.

Second, all the families have *equal shares* in the cooperative. Unity cannot be preserved unless there is a basic equality. That also includes the right of all households to elect their representative to the *executive committee* in which, according to law, all executive powers are vested.

The cooperative has an executive committee presided over by a chairman who is helped by a secretary. The members of the committee are elected by the cooperators. The chairman is elected by the committee members. The structures do exist. But the spirit which should animate them may not be present. What is needed is new culture, a new ideology.

The new ideology. Most of the questions asked so far express doubts as to how far the new ideology has been accepted. Are the cooperators still trapped in the superior/inferior polarity preached by casteism? More specifically, do the cooperators deep down in their hearts still wish to have been born into a higher caste? In other words, do they still admire the higher castes and somehow think less of themselves and their own brethren? Are they closer to accepting inferior *jatis* as their equals, and therefore ready to shed all types of discriminatory behaviour with them? Do they see private property and economic inequalities as a dividing factor and do they consequently prize common ownership as a means to unity and development?

These questions bring to the fore the problem of working with one caste alone. The initial facility in building up a community becomes a·block when trying to move from caste to class. On the other hand, the realisation of the practical advantages of cooperation, the newly developed interest in administrative, managerial and technical questions, and the new political awareness which makes them realise the importance of political alliances with other castes to survive in a democracy; all these factors make it easier to understand and to speak a modern political language which values class loyalties above the former narrow parochial ties. If the new values have been born the old ones have not yet died; the battle is on between the old feudal and new democratic ideals.

5

ACHIEVEMENTS OF
THE COOPERATIVE MOVEMENT

Concepts have been the main thrust of the previous pages. The time has come, first, to narrate happenings and, second to evaluate performances.

Table 5. Chronology of the Centre's Work in the Bhal.

1974	Course to 34 Vankar men in Ahmedabad.
1975	January: Course to Golana men in Ahmedabad. December: Course to Pandad men in Ahmedabad.
1976	December: Course to Vadgam men in Ahmedabad.
1977	January: Course to Rohini and Gudel men in Ahmedabad. February: Course to Vainej men in Ahmedabad. March-April: Socio-economic survey of the Bhal.
1978	Short courses in the villages to choose and launch the first cooperative: Galiana, Golana, Vainej, Vadgam. Selection of Vadgam and first agricultural experiments.
1979	August: Vadgam cooperative takes up afforestation. The nursery is started after the monsoon. December: First experimental transplantation.
1980	April: 70 acres transplanted. September: 24 acres added; gap-filling in 50 previously planted acres.
1981	Maintenance work in the cooperative. March: Course given to the Bharwads of Golana in Ahmedabad. April: Course to Vadgam women. December: All the Vankars in Pandad decide to set up a cooperative.
1982	January: Course to Varasada men in Ahmedabad.
1983	Gudel joins the cooperative movement. First attempts in Golana to incorporate all the Vankars into one of the two existing cooperatives.
1984	May: Course to Golana women. Valli and Vainej join the cooperative movement.

1985   Vadgam begins its cutting cycle earning Rs. 37,000 from seven acres.
Mithli joins the movement, though factional fights prevent the normal functioning of the cooperative.

1986   Four Vankars are killed in Golana. The community remains united and receives widespread support. Government becomes more sympathetic: a housing colony (115 houses) is sanctioned for Golana. The DRDA (District Rural Development Agency) sanctions grants to the Vadgam, Pandad, Gudel, Golana and Vainej Cooperatives totalling Rs. 1,022,152.
Khakhsar, Padra, and Rohini are given, on contract, the task of setting up nurseries. Vadgam and Golana cooperatives produce charcoal worth Rs. 188,000. The net income, Rs. 90,000, goes the loan towards repaying the loan.

1987   Rohini and Tamsa have their own cooperatives registered by the government. The former is given 100 acres and the latter 50 acres of land. Vadgam and Vainej also get 50 additional acres.
A second year of drought. No transplantation is possible.

1988   Good rains. Transplantation completed in all the cooperatives except Vadgam where factional fights have paralysed the cooperative.
Varasada sets up a fisheries cooperative to take up sweet water fish farming in the Kaneval Tank given on lease to the cooperative by the Fisheries Department. Indranaj asks for a similar cooperative.

Unless otherwise indicated the men or women of a particular village are Vankars.

Table 5 gives a bird's-eye view of the Centre's involvement in the Bhal, much of which has already been described. The initial years saw the Centre follow its earlier pedagogy of uninvolved education. From 1977 onwards the Centre began to doubt the efficacy of such education. Its members (then four) were reluctant to make any changes, at first; but the poor results of the educational efforts finally prevailed upon them to involve the Centre in the socio-economic lives of the scheduled castes. Two years later in 1979 the Vadgam cooperative decided to start a mesquite plantation on its land, laying the foundation of a sound economic enterprise.

According to the above table, there are now ten villages which have accepted the Centre's idea of a cooperative. The initial reluctance of Pandad and Golana has been overcome. Galiana stands alone outside the movement – although the pressure from below is mounting. This is in itself an achievement. However, let other less obvious but more important aspects be examined first.

The Cooperative as a University

The first achievement of our cooperatives is the educational work they do. It is also first in importance. Without the profound social and psychological changes which serious educational work alone can bring about, this movement will not achieve its ideal of radical change. These cooperatives, like most others, will end up by serving vested interests.

The educational work in the cooperatives is of two types: social and technical; the former is the educational wing's responsibility and the latter the technical wing's.

Social education. Social education forms the core of the courses described earlier. The aim is to bring about a critical understanding óf society. Self-respect, a determination to achieve unity and cooperation, and legitimate pride in one's own *jati*, are some of the concrete results expected from this new social awareness.

But an initial understanding is not enough to internalise the new values so powerfully as to make them always and everywhere opeiã-tional. Jealousies and power struggles, factional fights and betrayal of one's own brethren to the higher castes, selfish interests which jeopardise the smooth running of the cooperative, friction and the inevitable discouragement of daily life, all these factors tend to obscure and even push into the background the insights gained from the courses. The beauty of the cooperative is that it provides a plat-form and an opportunity to make social awareness bear upon the more down-to-earth and concrete realities which affect the in-dividual closely. When this is done the process of internalisation takes place much more effectively. Examples will clarify both the end of this social education and its process.

In early 1983 the chairman of the Vadgam cooperative requested the Centre's staff to advance a loan of Rs. 80,000 to buy a plot of land which the *sarpanch* wanted to sell. It was meant for a group of individuals, ready to mortgage the land to the Centre until the loan was paid back. The Centre's representative replied: "The Centre does not help individuals, but the whole community. Is this land going to be for the whole community? If not, you are creating divisions."

Having failed with the Centre, the group approached another voluntary organisation with better luck. A section of the village now had land. As against the joy of those who had been given land, there was the bitterness of those who had been disappointed. There was a fight, there was division.

Unfortunately, the Centre's Trainee had taken a very active part in securing the loan and in having the land given to some individuals. He was taken to task:

> "The whole operation has divided the community; the main beneficiary has been the *sarpanch* who has contrived both to obtain a good price for land which government would have taken away in any case, and to have one faction indebted to him. This has forced the other faction into the hands of another high caste. It is they who now control you all. On the other hand, the fact that you have identified yourself so much with one faction in the village disqualifies you from being an educational worker."

He readily accepted the last point and submitted his resignation.

In a subsequent meeting the Centre clarified its stand in answer to persistent queries. "The Centre is opposed to the land deal because it divides the community. True, every cooperator has the right to secure things for himself from wherever he can. Such efforts would not be opposed; but, at the same time, care should be taken to avoid or minimise their divisive effect and their impact on the working of the cooperative."

There was a deeper issue, of course. What model of society had we accepted? Capitalism with its stress on private property, individual enrichment, competition to be the most powerful person in the community? Or, were we stressing unity, cooperation, mutual support? It is easy to uphold these ideals during training sessions in distant Ahmedabad; but when the temptation to enrich ourselves comes, then are we ready to stand by our values?

Controversy over this incident raged unabated in Vadgam for more than a year. The election of the chairman became the external symbol of the factional fight. Work in the cooperative came to a standstill. High caste interference with the Vankar *jati* increased notoriously. It was the poorer families who brought back sanity and common sense. They needed the grain given to them by the food-for-work programme of the cooperative. What did the Centre do all the while? The 1984 Report explains it:

. . : the Centre stood firm on its basic principles: unity comes first. The good of the community is more important than the enrichment of individuals. This stand brought on the Centre the wrath of many cooperators. Feelings were running high and communication became difficult. For a long time our man in Vadgam did nothing but listen to them all, taking note of what they said but remaining silent all the while. It was not so much what the Centre could say as what the people were willing to see that would make the difference. There are certain wounds that time alone can heal. Patience and understanding are more important to the educator than articulate speech and well reasoned arguments. That was the right pedagogy: the eloquence of silence, the loving concern of patience and what makes it all possible, faith that people can see things for themselves at their own time.

It was a painful experience; but it resulted in greater awareness of both the need for and the difficulty of achieving unity.

Individual greed is an obstacle to unity; so are the power needs of cooperative officials.

The Vainej cooperative became a reality during 1985 mainly due to the efforts of two men. They went from house to house, explaining the advantages of the cooperative. They moved from government office to office to have the cooperative registered. Having done all the spadework they, understandably, felt very possessive about it. The Centre's educational officer kept on insisting that the cooperative belonged to *all* and had to be managed, as far as possible, by *all*. Most people in Vainej were quicker to understand this principle than the "founders" of the cooperative. When the former insisted on their voice being heard and their votes counted, the reaction of the latter was instantaneous and fulminating:

"Who has done all the work? Who will do it in the future? If that is what you want, you run it!"

The others were cowed down. The educational officer, gently at first, tried to persuade these two individuals to place their faith in the community. When that failed, he was forced to tell them all:

"Remember the Centre's conditions. The cooperative is for all and it must be run by all. If this condition is forfeited, the Centre has no choice but to leave this village."

These words did not have the desired impact. So, the educational officer left.

Unlike Vadgam, Vainej was quicker to call the Centre back. The surprising thing was the impact that this symbolic gesture had on these two young Turks. In their own words: "In practice we did not have much respect for our own people. That is why we wanted to run the whole thing ourselves. We did not trust the others. But you are right. We cannot have self-respect without, at the same time, respecting our brethren, and respect means taking them seriously."

Another very important aspect of this social education is the effort being constantly made to keep the channels of communication open. First it is necessary to explain to all the cooperators the running of the cooperative: how much money has been spent and why, what steps have been taken in the plantation: in bunding, transplantation, drainage, felling of trees, water-harvesting techniques, etc.; how much work this has generated; how many families have benefited from it. Knowledge is power. And knowledge about the cooperative means power over it. Knowledge of the work of their own cooperative cements the participation and commitment of its workers.

If the cooperators must know what the cooperative does, the cooperative must know what its ordinary members think. It is necessary, therefore, to have the officials of the cooperative listen to the people: their needs, their complaints, their perceptions. Responsiveness to the ordinary members ensures the involvement of all the people – and not of just a few individuals. When there is a free flow of information, manipulation becomes difficult. The task of listening to each cooperator is initially taken up by the Centre's personnel; but, sooner or later, it must devolve on the cooperative itself. The Centre trains several people from each cooperative, its *educational counterparts*, to take up this work. Success in this educational effort will be achieved when the involvement of the whole community in the cooperative is a reality.

Conflict is part and parcel of every human institution. It cannot be avoided. The institution has to learn to deal with it. Therefore, dealing effectively with conflict is another item in the social education programme. This sometimes demands working with the executive committee of the cooperative, sometimes with the traditional leaders, sometimes with the whole village which is engulfed in a factional war. The ideals of unity and cooperation are not easily learnt. Refresher courses are organised for the whole village either in the village itself, or in Daheda or in Ahmedabad.

Technical education. The cooperative is also an economic enterprise. It demands very specific skills to carry out its various tasks. These, too, must be taught. And, indeed, the efficiency of the cooperative depends on its day-to-day administration. The committee members and the chairman are not business executives. They are more like the board of directors adopting general policy and approving yearly plans and budgets. The implementation is left to paid personnel. There must be sufficient numbers of people who *can* perform these tasks, or else the cooperative will depend too much on a few individuals. This would severely restrict its freedom. Table 6 lists all the tasks to be performed which are part of the course syllabus. It is difficult to organise all the activities. Outside help may be necessary. But the implementation of each task is easily learnt and practised − a new learning which is also a new qualification acquired in this "de-schooled university," where the teacher/taught dichotomy resolves itself into one learning community. The Centre's experts have learnt as much as their local counterparts − and this common effort has not been a mere academic, or irrelevant, exercise, but an answer to very concrete problems. The conceptual power of the expert is complemented by his counterpart's knowledge and experience of local conditions.

Table 6 gives an idea of the syllabus covered. How far have the students learnt their lessons? By 1988 six cooperatives had 475 acres of land afforested as shown in Table 9. Varasada has initiated a movement of diversification from forestry into fisheries. All this work has been done by the Vankars of the Bhal with the help of two other Vankars from the Charotar (one subsequently left the place), and the overall supervision of the Centre's agricultural manager. The Centre does employ one outsider in both the marketing and the distribution of food-for-work. The whole accounts office at Daheda, on the other hand, is manned by local Vankars, guided by the Centre's financial manager and its accountant.

As the lower supervisors gather experience − so far they have done it reasonably fast − they soon qualify to take up more responsible tasks. Some are now being prepared to take up the administration of the proposed federation. In conclusion, the great educational effort at the technical level seems to have been both important and successful.

Table 6: **Tasks of the Cooperative**

1. *Production.*

   a. *Physical care of the land*: bunding, drainage system,
   water harvesting measures.

   b. *Production:*
   Nursery: preparation of site, seeds, purchase of plastic bags, provision of watering facilities, sowing, preparation of beds, replacement of failures.
   Transplantation: preparation of pits in equidistant rows; transportation of saplings from nursery, planting of saplings, watering, gap-filling.
   Harvesting: tree felling, wood cutting, charcoal making.

   c. *Labour*: recruitment of labour according to executive committee's guidelines, supervision of work, fixing of wages.

2. *Finances*: keeping monthly accounts, preparation of coming month's budget, presentation of the budget to the finance committee and to the Daheda office. Receipt and expenditure of cash.

3. *Marketing*: [At present the Centre surveys the market, bargains with traders, secures permits from the Forest Department, arranges for transportation]. Preparation of stocks (firewood or charcoal) according to orders received, loading of truck, weighing, delivery to the client, paying the tolls, and receiving payment.

The previous pages have shown that the cooperative offers a structure very similar to a university where, through action, the cooperators learn new skills and imbibe new values. It imparts both social and technical education. The two have been explained separately to highlight the vastness of the educational effort.

Values and technology, however, cannot be separated because technology and management are not value-free. It is precisely because the structure of the cooperative accepts the values of the movement that education becomes possible. In this *new* structure new knowledge can be acquired and practised. Like the plantation itself, it is an oasis in an otherwise stifling atmosphere, an oasis within the Vankar *jati* and in the village itself. It defends the lowest in the caste hierarchy from the constant affirmation of caste ideology. Indeed, the cooperative is its negation, for it frees the former untouchables from their masters and it takes away from the latter their most powerful weapon, economic power. In this free structure the new values can be affirmed without fear of economic or other types of retaliation.

The Cooperative as a New Social Structure

The cooperative is a new structure, a *Gesellschaft*, "one characterised by . . . contractualism and proceeding from volition or sheer interest rather than from the complex affective states, habit, and traditions that underlie a *Gemeinschaft*" (Nisbet, 1966: 74).*[1] The cooperative is different from and yet not opposed to the *Gemeinschaft*; reactionary attitudes can easily be revived and factional fights cannot be avoided because the traditional leaders still wield absolute power. It is a new structure which looks at the future without denying the past – *Gesellschaft* and *Gemeinschaft* walking hand in hand. Yet, both preserve their distinct identities: the latter is sacral, traditional, closely linked to caste ideology, to "a mythical past, a total way of life, a secure identity," while the former is "flexible, future-oriented, secularised and limited in its scope" (see Cox, 1966: 175); the latter views the present in terms of the past while the former studies the present to prepare a better future, dealing with concrete problems and realistic solutions; in the latter, a person's position in society is determined by birth, in the former it is determined by compétence and the ability to carry out specific tasks.

The cooperative as *Gesellschaft* makes limited claims on its members and can easily be accepted by all. And yet the cooperative is a call to radical change. In this ambivalence lies both the strength and the weakness of this venture – its possibilities and its dangers. The *possibility* of a smooth, almost imperceptible onward movement away from caste ideology, from ascription and privilege to freedom, rationality and inner worth. This smooth change is both a break with the past and a continuation of the best of its traditions. It is a break which is not a *total* revolution, without its dangers: anomie, chaos, and the unavoidable return to autocracy. The *Gesellschaft* may revert to the *Gemeinschaft*, the new assets may be sucked away to strengthen old privilege – a disquieting thought, a frustrating possibility. But then life is a risk.

---

1. * Gessellschaft, according to the German Sociologist F. Tonnies, is a group of people characterised by a high degree of individualism, impersonality, contractualism, and proceeding from sheer interest rather than from a complex of affective states, habits, traditions.
   Gemeinschaft is a community encompassing all forms of relationship characterised by a high degree of personal intimacy, emotional depth, moral commitment, social cohesion and continuity in time.

In this new structure of *de-schooling* the learning process is possible because the topics are not distant or abstract, the teacher is not raised on a podium, the students are not passive listeners. There is no alienation from self, community or village, no flight away from the barren fields, no separation between thought and action, trainer and trainee; but a constant dialogue between the agricultural experience, the personal, intimate knowledge of the local farmers, on the one hand, and the concepts (science deals with abstractions) of the technical expert, on the other. It is a common search, a real transfer of technology which applies the findings of the posh research centres to the humble wastelands of backward areas.

It is also a dialogue between modern managerial practices and the old traditional way of running a *jati* group. The former can organise a village into a competitive production unit and federate several villages into an efficient marketing business; the latter can control the *jati*, have it work with discipline and thus enhance productivity; the former can introduce and teach more relevant technology while the latter can have it thoroughly examined to check its suitability and then have it accepted without reservation by all the *jati* members. There is scientific knowledge in the former, there is wisdom in the latter. There is managerial knowhow in the former, there is worldly *savoir faire* in the latter. Modern technology in the former, common sense in the latter. The cooperative is the university where modern knowledge and local experience meet and dialogue about the possibilities which the present offers to build a more just, more loving and, consequently, happier future.

The foregoing pages have explained an educational project which started very crudely in 1974, adopted the cooperative movement in 1979, perfected its structures by 1982 and expanded its activities to ten villages by 1988. But the educational process itself and its success depend on the realisation of the other aims of the cooperative.

The Socio-economic Goals of the Cooperative

Social evils result from unjust economic structures. Unless the latter are changed the former cannot be rooted out. Previous economic structures made the Vankars economically dependent on the Rajputs. A new one has now been set up to make the whole Vankar *jati* economically self-sufficient. Has the cooperative achieved this goal?

Table 7 lists the amounts of loans given to each cooperative. The implication of its figures is in sharp contrast to those in Table 2 which also show indebtedness. The latter is the indebtedness of individuals who have obtained money by binding themselves to work for low wages in the fields of the moneylender. The former is money obtained because the project is judged sound by funding agencies. This must be stressed. Funding agencies may refuse a loan to a cooperative and may give it to the Centre. This does not mean that they give it to the Centre; what they want is a guarantee that the money *will* be spent on the proposed project and according to the approved budget. When an institution like the Centre asks for a grant, the funding agency trusts that the above conditions will be fulfilled and sanctions it. Were the Centre to ask for some other project which does not make so much sense as the cooperative, its request might be turned down. The loans shown in Table 7 prove the credit-worthiness of the venture in which there are two partners, the Centre and the cooperators. When the latter's seriousness is well established the former's presence is not required.

Table 7 : **Investment in the Cooperatives (Up to December 1988)**

| Village | Acres of Land | | Financial Help (BSC) | | | DRDA |
	Total	Plantation	Grants*	Loans Outstanding	Paid	Grants
Vadgam	232	125	230,930	46,685	126,926	210,005
Pandad	578	179	395,325	126,870	16,588	314,752
Golana	147	75	189,560	158,120	131,850	271,658
Gudel	85	4	103,200	44,020	798	51,116
Valli	34	29	93,618	74,709	18,988	—
Vainej	83	68	210,672	13,080	23,150	83,921
Rohini	100	4	23,793	3,500		—
Tamsa	50	—	—	—	—	—
Mithli	67	8	26,505	26,326	179	
	13,76	492	1,273,603	493,310	318,479	931,452

* This consists of food for work. It has been calculated by multiplying the total number of mandays by Rs. 7.

Such big loans did frighten the cooperators. To allay their fears, the Centre made a rule that the cooperative would not have to repay any loan if the venture failed. The Centre hands over the money as the need arises. The above loans, therefore, have already been spent.

It has to be noted, however, that the money has not been utilised exclusively for the plantations, as Table 7 may perhaps indicate. The number of acres which the cooperative owns and those under cultivation are shown in the table as the most tangible example of the economic activities undertaken so far. However, every cooperative needs money to pay for its administrative expenses and the salaries of its permanent employees. Moreover, about Rs. 150,000 have been spent on agriculture. If these expenses are deducted, it costs an average of Rs. 4,700 to reclaim an acre of saline land (Annual Report, 1985-87).

Apart from administrative expenses and expenses on agriculture the main items of expenditure include the purchase of equipment, fertilisers, seeds and other material and the payment of wages for the work done in the maintenance of the plantation, the preparation of the nursery, the transplantation work, etc. As far as possible, wages are paid with grain and oil under the food-for-work programme. This practice has been followed to pay for all the physical work on the various plantations, like bunding, pit digging etc.. Initially, however, the transplantation and gap-filling operations were paid for in cash (that is why early cooperatives like Vadgam and Pandad show such big loans); but later on they were also brought under the food-for-work programme. The amount of grain and oil given is shown in Table 7, as a grant: the calculation has been made by multiplying each manday (corresponding to 4 kg of grain and 100 grams of oil) by Rs. 7. But for this food-for-work programme, it would have been impossible to bring all these highly degraded lands under cultivation, as it will be explained later.

Government realises the importance both of reclaiming wastelands and of re-afforestation, that is why the District Rural Development Agency gives a grant of Rs. 1,500 per acre under a scheme called social forestry. The total amount thus far received is also given in Table 7. Table 8 gives all the details of the grants received under this scheme.

The Golana cooperative earned some money from agriculture. Pandad had maintained the central nursery, during 1983-84, which earned the cooperative about Rs. 8,000 from the sale of saplings to other cooperatives. Apart from these, the main source of income has been the sale of firewood and charcoal by the Golana (Rs. 122,000) and Vadgam (Rs. 97,800) cooperatives. While the income from Vadgam is the result of the cooperative's efforts, in Golana there was a natural plantation. During 1983-84 part of it and in 1986 most

of it was cut and charcoal made. Vadgam had seven acres cut in
early 1985 and about 20 acres in 1986.

Table 8: Cooperative-wise Receipts of Grants under DRDA (1-4-86 to 31-12-88)

Village	Grant		Expenditure		
	Cash	Coupons	Cash	Coupons	Total
Vadgam	173,985	94,347	131,049	78,956	210,005
Golana	188,663	103,509	177,222	94,436	271,658
Gudel	31,525	23,152	31,350	19,766	51,116
Pandad	209,625	113,321	201,430	113,322	314,752
Vainej	54,500	29,525	54,395	29,525	83,920
Total	658,298	363,854	595,446	336,005	931,451

The above shows that the cooperatives in the Bhal have
mobilised resources either from within or outside to pay wages to all
their cooperators during the slack season. In other words, individual
cooperators have received *wages* which were not available before.
What has been the impact of this additional income on the Vankars?
A higher income does not necessarily bring about economic
self-sufficiency. If the expenditure increases at a higher rate than the
income or, in other words, if people live beyond their means,
indebtedness will continue to be a problem.

On the negative side, the cooperative which has remained a
Gessellschaft, has not made any effort to cut down on social customs
like marriages and funerals which still force people into the hands of
the moneylender. However, these occasions are not an everyday
occurrence and, money being more readily available within the
Vankar *jati*, the dependence on the Rajputs is not felt as much as
before. Avoidable expenses are still the medical bills which the
present health system imposes on them. A good community health
programme could bring down these bills by as much as nine-tenths
in each household. Much money could also be saved if the
cooperative could start its own shops. At present, in the villages,
shop prices are 50 per cent higher than those in Cambay. However,
the villagers can now buy against ready cash which is more easily
available.

On the positive side, the availability of work all the year round
has freed many families from the necessity of working in the fields of
high caste people as share-croppers which used to be a sure road to

indebtedness. Freedom from indebtedness has also increased their bargaining power during the peak agricultural season. They can now exact higher wages.

All in all, the Vankars today are not forced to bend their knees to the Rajputs. Most of the time, now, they work in their own fields, because the cooperative is theirs. In the words of a cooperator, "The greatest benefit of the cooperative has been that my wife need not go to work any longer in the fields of the Rajput." Evidently, it is easier to enhance one's self-image and to internalise values of self-respect when one works in one's own fields and can thus preserve the honour of his wife. It is easier to preserve one's own dignity and sense of self-worth when one does not have to beg for money because one has a regular income, the salary of the work in the community's enterprise. This is precisely the social goal of the cooperative.

The Cooperative as a Business Enterprise

The performance of the cooperative as a business can be measured in economic terms: the creation of assets and the relation of assets to liabilities in the long run.

Table 9: **Cooperative-wise Forestry Assets up to 1988**

Village	Acres			
	Total	Planted	Established	Productive
Vadgam	232	150	125	25 now 50 after 2 years 50 after 4 years
Pandad	578	214	179	50 after 4 years 50 after 8 years
Golana	147	110	75	25 now 50 after 4 years
Gudel	85	50	4	—
Valli	34	34	29	25 after 3 years
Vainej	83	68	63	33 after 3 years 30 after 5 years
Total	1159	626	475	388

Table 9 shows that this cooperative movement has already created 388 acres of forestry assets. Golana has retained 20 acres of good land for agriculture. The manner in which these assets were created bears witness to the vitality of the cooperative as a business enterprise. The land on which the plantation has been established was earlier a useless, barren tract where not even grass would grow. The following difficulties which characterised this soil had to be dealt with (1981 Report):

1. *Low hydraulic conductivity* leads either to waterlogging in low-lying areas or to excessive runoff in the rest resulting in the waste of valuable rain water during the monsoon and water stress during summer.

2. *Shattered soil structure* causes compaction of soil which prevents adequate aeration and greatly reduces the water-holding and cation exchange capacity. This is the characteristic of alkaline soils only and is brought about by excess deposition of sodium ions. A few patches of such land are visible in Vadgam and many more in Pandad and Gudel.

3. *Salt deposits in the root zone* raise the osmotic potential of soil solution to levels higher than that of the plant solution resulting in "physiological drought." The plant begins to wilt due to inadequate moisture in the system. Furthermore, the inflow of ions from the soil solution is also checked, causing inadequate nutrition. This is the typical situation of saline soils in which the soil structure is preserved but there is absence of moisture because of semi-arid climatic conditions.

Insistence on proper planting methods was the first answer to these difficulties, but this did not bring any noticeable improvement to the initial 35 per cent survival rate. Moisture, not the planting method, was the critical factor. Physical improvement of the land was a heavy but inevitable expense. A number of improvements were carried out. Bunds or embankments around small plots were made to retain the monsoon water; straight, parallel *trenches* dug up all along the plot, heaping the soil by the side to form a long straight ridge on to which the saplings could be transplanted; *pits* dug by the side of each plant to harvest rain water; *drains* made to prevent waterlogging.

The problem with these massive operations is the initial investment which may prove a permanent liability. This difficulty was overcome with the timely help of the food-for-work programme. The US Catholic Relief Services was running this programme from its Bombay regional office and offered us, through the Kaira Social Service Society (a Catholic voluntary organisation working in the district) 10,000 mandays (the equivalent of Rs. 100,000 in 1985 prices). From 1981 onwards, grain and oil were directly shipped to the Centre to improve the plantations and the amount was increased to 30,000 mandays a year. The number of mandays up to December 1988 amounts to 182,000. The grain is a gift of the American government; the transportation charges up to Cambay are borne by the Food Corporation of India. It is only the transportation from Cambay to the site of distribution which has to be paid for by the clients.

The food-for-work programme has been severely criticised because it creates dependence, and because it feeds the poor to increase the wealth of the rich. The manner in which food-for-work was used in the Bhal cooperatives has neither created dependence – on the contrary it has created assets and therefore independence – nor has it served to enrich the rich – on the contrary, it has helped the poor free themselves from the clutches of the moneylender.

The result of these improvements and the close watch, maintained on the plants, looking out for the symptoms of moisture stress – the Centre's small tanker pulled by a tractor has saved many a plant – has been a dramatic increase in the survival rate from the dismal 35 to an encouraging 70 per cent. This has, in effect, halved the cost per plant.

Mere survival may be a nice experiment, it may also have some ecological advantages; but it is not enough. Without vigorous growth the plantation will not make commercial sense. The cooperative needs a steady income if it aspires to become a business enterprise and eventually to reach its social goals. Table 9 shows that there are already 388 acres which can become commercially viable within eight years.

Vadgam had a debt of Rs. 173,610, but by 1987 it had repaid Rs. 126,926 leaving an outstanding loan of Rs. 46,685 only. This repayment came from the earnings of the cutting of six acres in early 1985 and a subsequent cutting of about 20 acres in 1986. Therefore, before the whole plantation is cut for the first time, this loan should be cleared completely. Thus, every subsequent cutting should generate a surplus.

The projection from these experiments is that an acre may yield an average Rs. 4,000 gross income, providing Rs. 2,500 in wages to the cooperators and a net income of Rs. 1,300 to the cooperative. Pandad can easily turn 100 out of its 578 acres into a commercial plantation. From 1986 onwards all the efforts in the plantation have been concentrated on improving the best plots rather than on increasing the planted acreage. The cost in Pandad has been lower than it has in Vadgam because of the improved methods followed. The loan of Rs. 126,870 taken from the Centre should not be difficult to repay.

In the case of Gudel, the plantation has not been established due to technical reasons. The existence of a high brackish water-table has been the main constraint. An attempt to grow paddy had to be abandoned because the source of irrigation proved to be unreliable. Gudel does not have a large Vankar population. The small plots of land owned by some of them have become a good source of income because of the Mahi canal which irrigates the village. As a result the economic situation of the Vankar *jati* has improved noticeably.

The insistence on assets and liabilities is, in a way, an academic exercise; because the Centre has made it quite clear that its loans are not liabilities. The cooperative is bound to return the loan *only* if the venture succeeds. This exercise is, however, necessary. The objection raised by some that these cooperatives will last only as long as the outsider keeps pouring money in must be clearly answered. The cooperative is not a charitable institution, but a business enterprise. Therefore it has to make business sense. The ability to mobilise financial resources is part of this sense. True, people give money out of a social concern. Therefore, it is easier to receive financial help for the cooperative than it would be for an ordinary firm. It is precisely this facility which implies the danger of creating dependence. But, after some time, the cooperatives will not need outside help, because they have used the present resources to create permanent assets.

How much money has this cooperative movement been able to secure? Misereor (agency of the German Catholic Bishops), through the Indo-German Social Service Society of New Delhi, gave the Centre a grant of Rs. 1,200,000 which paid the salaries of the staff for three years, provided the cooperatives with a working capital, bought the land and paid for buildings at the site of the proposed federation of cooperatives in Daheda (warehouse, offices, living quarters for the technical personnel and a multipurpose hall) and took care of all the expenses of our educational programme.

As mentioned earlier Catholic Relief Services, Bombay, provided the grain and oil under its food-for-work programme.

The cooperatives have also done creditably well at improving productivity. The initial attrition rate in the transplantation work was lowered from the unaffordable 65 to a reasonable 30 per cent, as mentioned earlier. Productivity has also improved in the field. The cooperators, accustomed to work in the exploiter's field, had developed the understandable picaresque of digging less and claiming more, specially under the food-for-work programme. The supervisors complained and were shouted down by the workers. The practice was discussed, first in Vadgam where the Centre encountered it initially and later in the executive committees of the other cooperatives. Pandad, ever the toughest bargainer, refused to see reason. The Centre was forced to stop the food-for-work programme; but when it did recommence, after six months, a new attitude and a new culture had been introduced. People had realised that cheating one's own cooperative and the agencies which helped it, did not make sense.

As mentioned earlier, the decision taken by the Centre in Vadgam to have the executive committee appoint its own supervisors and impose sanctions to curb indiscipline proved very effective. However, the Centre's agricultural manager and team do carry out overall supervisory functions to ensure the highest productivity.

Marketing is another area which has demanded much attention and effort on the part of the technical personnel. These efforts have borne fruit, as Tables 10 and 11 show. Vadgam sold its first consignment in mid-1982 in an effort to test the market. The operation is summed up in Table 10. The price realised at that time was a meagre 17 paise per kilogram, a paltry net profit of 9 paise per kg. As compared with these, the sale of charcoal in 1985 saw a dramatic increase of Re. 1.24 per kg. in the price realised and an increase of 30 paise in the net profit per kg of charcoal. Subsequent sales further improved the net profit per kg of charcoal by another 32 to 35 paise, raising it to 73 paise per kg.

Table 10 : **Income and Expenditure in the Sale of 90 Trees**

Income		Expenditure	
8,940 kgs* of fire-wood X Rs.0.20	1,788.00	Cutting expenses	355.00
		Transportation	360.00
Less: Commission			
@ 5%	−89.40	Other	111.00
Brokerage	−10.00		
		Total	826.00
		Net profit	862.60
	1,688.60		1,688.60

*   The actual weight was 9,440 kgs; but the trader deducted 500 kg as his own profit.
The actual price realised, therefore, was Re. 0.17 per kg., or Rs. 1,688.60 : 9,440.
The net profit Re. 0.09 per kg.

Table 11 : **Charcoal Manufacture and Sale. Golana and Vadgam**

Year and Place	Charcoal (Tons)	Gross Income (Rupees)	Price per Ton (Rupees)	Net Income (Rupees)	Note
Golana					
1984	26.84	37,873.38	1,411.08	10,462.69	(1)
1986	56.68	84,932.40	1,494.23	40,520.45	(2)
Vadgam					
1986	64.29	96,161.30	1,495.74	46,892.42	(3)

(1) Price realised: Re. 1.41 per kg. Net profit: Re. 0.39 per kg.
(2) Price realised: Re. 1.49 per kg. Net profit: Re. 0.71 per kg.
(3) Price realised: Re. 1.49 per kg. Net profit: Re. 0.73 per kg.

Prosopis firewood has a very short shelf life. It has to be sold and consumed very soon after cutting. Again, transportation charges are high, taking into consideration the relative cheapness of this commodity. The best solution to these problems is to prepare charcoal from the wood. Since charcoal can be stored and sold when market conditions fetch a better price, its manufacture is advisable when there are no clients ready to buy the firewood on site. It is also advisable when there is unemployment because it does provide employment.

Golana was the first cooperative to manufacture charcoal on a large scale during 1984; the result of this operation is given in Table

11 which also gives the results of a subsequent exercise in 1986 in which Vadgam also took part.

Even if firewood sometimes yields a higher income, charcoal-making may be more desirable because of the wages it generates (21 paise out of the total expenditure of 27 paise spent on turning one kg of wood into charcoal are spent on wages given to the cooperators).

Summary

The management of the cooperative movement seems to be performing satisfactorily:

1 It has created assets through the mobilisation and wise use of *financial* and other resources.

2 It has brought about the transfer of beneficial *technology*.

3 It has kept up its search for suitable *markets*. And, finally,

4 It has conducted intensive *training* of *local talent* to promote persons to higher technical and administrative tasks.

It has protected the created assets and preserved them for the benefit of all the members of a scheduled caste. This economic goal guarantees economic self-sufficiency, the foundation of a new set of more equitable and just social relations which uphold the dignity and self-respect of the individual.

6

THE FUTURE OF THE MOVEMENT

Apart from the unpredictability which the cooperatives share with any other business enterprise, the future of this movement may well depend both on its ability to develop mutually helpful ties with other *jatis*, and on the soundness of its relationship with the Centre. Relations with the former will determine whether the Vankar *jati* is integrated into the social and political life of the Bhal; while relations with the latter will show whether this movement is nothing but the creation of the Centre or has the potential to become an autonomous reality.

The Vankar Cooperative Movement and Other Jatis

Vadgam. High caste people did not give much importance to the cooperative when it started, because chances of success had seemed minimal. The harassment the Centre had to face was the result of the ordinary resentment some high caste individuals have towards outsiders who work with the scheduled castes. Thus, for example the *sarpanch's* foreman did try to intimidate the Centre's staff. He was treated courteously but firmly and soon desisted from further provocation. The *sarpanch* himself, wealthy, intelligent and well-connected with influential people at both the taluka and district levels, made it clear to all that he would not interfere in what he called the Centre's work. This attitude of the *sarpanch* who was also the undisputed leader of the Rajputs, the dominant caste, led to an era of peaceful coexistence as far as the cooperative and the Rajputs were concerned.

A possible quarrel with the Bharwads (shepherds), who had illegally occupied part of the cooperative land, was avoided by allowing them to keep it on two conditions: first, the tax for that piece of land should be paid by them and, second, they should allow the Vankars to work peacefully on the rest of the land. Another possible source of friction was the Bharwads' cattle which are a menace to young plants. The Vankars appointed a respected Bharwad as watchman of the plantation to keep the cattle away. Much friction was thus avoided and damage, too.

The staff of the Centre was ostracised socially, since it was working not only for, but also with, a scheduled caste. However, as the work of the cooperative became more and more impressive, most people started looking at the Centre with respect. Indeed, it would not have been difficult —but for lack of personnel —to work with intermediate *jatis* in Vadgam and in the rest of the Bhal.

In *Vainej* too the Bharwads had illegally occupied the land given by government to the Vankars, as part of its policy to help the scheduled castes. There was less land; but it was much better. It was all in their hands. For a long time the Vankars refused to accept such a gift from government to the irritation of revenue officers who could not close the file and who, worse still, had to explain things to their superiors in Gandhinagar, the state capital. After much prodding from the officials and discussions with the Centre, a decision was finally taken to form a cooperative and to take up work in the fields in spite of Bharwad opposition which is notoriously ruthless.

The elders had raised objections: they did not know how to face the Bharwads. But the younger leadership persuaded them to leave the village on the day when work would start. The younger men knew how to deal with the Bharwads. The appointed day arrived. The young leaders went to the cooperative fields. They were alone. The Bharwads had bribed the other Vankars to work in Bharwad fields. Youth does not give up easily, however. The young Vankars found a way to force the other Vankars back into the cooperative's fields.

The Bharwads, having failed with the carrot, or bribe, now resorted to the stick — literally. Our young leaders did not want a fight, much less martyrdom. If a good strategic retreat is the hallmark of a good general, their leadership lived up to the best military traditions. Off they went to Cambay to lodge a complaint with government at whose insistence the fields had been taken. Let government do the fighting. The presence of the police in Vainej and their persuasion made it easier to reach an agreement: the Bharwads would appeal through the courts against the revenue officers and if the appeal was upheld the fields would be returned to them. No compensation would be demanded for the work done. In the meantime, the Vankars would be allowed peaceful possession of the land.

This compromise with the Bharwads allowed the cooperators to work untroubled in the fields.

The cooperative movement has consistently relied on government help to settle disputes. Legislation, the presence of fair bureaucrats, the fact that scheduled caste persons have begun to man important posts in the civil service at the taluka level, the political clout that scheduled caste MLAs have with the Chief Minister, and the fact that a city-based organisation is behind the movement —all these factors have so far helped the cooperatives to have their legitimate rights defended by taluka officers.

Pandad people are not precisely meek and humble of heart; neither is peace a priority in their minds. Ironically, the costly infighting of the Rajputs had put Pandad in contact with the Centre, even before its involvement with the Vankars. A young Rajput studying at St. Xavier's asked the Centre to give a course to his people. He had heard of the Centre's successful efforts with the Patels of Kubadthal, and in his eagerness to help his people tried to organise a course. That was in May 1974. The impact of this course has been described elsewhere – (Heredero 1977: 102-3):

> The 7th course was not successful due to our inexperience. We had not yet realised that heterogeneous caste groups were very difficult to handle and in this group we had Rajputs and Scheduled Castes. But this was not the only handicap. Our contact man in the village, a student of the college, did most of the recruiting work through the Yuvak Mandal (Youth Association) of which he was a leading member. This association did an excellent job in recruiting younger people but failed to attract the more influential members of their own caste. The course remained mainly a Yuvak Mandal's activity and failed to have much impact with the rest of the village.

Being so deeply divided, the Rajputs could hardly wage a serious battle against the Vankars. Relations, all the same, remained strained. The practice of hiding away a bullock cart and then asking for a ransom, and the Vankars' fight to put an end to it, have been mentioned earlier. In 1984 a Rajput youth molested a Vankar girl. The youth, humiliated by his father who had taken him to task, saw an opportunity to take revenge during a cricket match between Rajputs and Vankars. He started a fight against the latter who, as usual, preferred to lodge a complaint with the police rather than fight. It was sheer strategy and not the desire for peace which moved them.

On their way to Cambay, the Vankars planned their next move:

"If we complain of what has happened today," one said, "the police are not going to be very impressed."

"That is right," added another, "and they will take no action. In the end the Rajputs will laugh at us."

"We must dramatise the event. Why don't we say that the fight started because one of our women was molested by a Rajput youth? After all, that is true. It did take place some time back. The Rajputs will not be able to deny it."

After a moment of silence a third person smiled, looked around and said, "Let us make sure that we impress the police officers. In our complaint we must mention that the Rajputs used a country pistol."

"But they didn't," shouted two people at the same time.

"You are right. But tell me one thing: don't they have a pistol?"

"Yes, they have."

"Do they have a licence?"

"No, they don't."

"Well, you know how the authorities frown upon the possession of unlicensed weapons. They will object more to that than to their beating us."

Thus, the Vankars cleverly concocted a case: a fight (just happened) over an attempted rape (happened earlier) with the use of a country pistol (not used, but in the possession of the Rajputs). As they had anticipated, the mention of the pistol raised the eyebrows of the police officer. He just refused to mention that in the complaint. (Probably, he was afraid that an enquiry would be ordered against him for having allowed unlicensed weapons in the area under his jurisdiction.) His reluctance further emboldened the Vankars who even threatened to alert the state capital. The hard-pressed officer sought a way out of this impasse by convincing the Rajputs that this was a very difficult case and that the best thing they could do was to pay the Vankars a compensation. The Rajputs accepted in principle and bargained with the Vankars about the exact sum which was finally fixed at Rs. 8,500.

The Vankars accepted both the money and the request of the police to omit the mention of illicit arms. But, to everybody's surprise and Rajput outrage at their being outwitted, they insisted on having a complaint registered against the Rajputs, which the police finally had to do.

So much commotion at police headquarters could not pass unnoticed. Political parties and correspondents of the local newspapers came to enquire. The Vankars told them about the attempted rape which made a good story for the papers. Within a few days several newspapers published the incident, complaining about deteriorating moral standards – and government inaction. Local politicians visited Pandad to show their sympathy to the victims, good propaganda for their party, – and so did harassed government officials who had to prepare the inevitable report.

The Vankars were in the limelight and the Rajputs were forced to lie low. But soon the outsiders forgot Pandad, and the Rajputs began to mount their offensive. Their first attack was on the cooperative's fields where they did some damage. The Centre was alerted and informed of the previous events.

The Centre could not approve the behaviour of the Vankars. Neither could it allow the Rajputs to do further damage to the fields of the cooperative. The matter was discussed with the executive committee of the cooperative which decided to make an official complaint to the police. This was the second case against the Rajputs registered with the Cambay police: the other, the case of rape against the Rajput youth, was still pending.

The Rajput elders counselled moderation. "The times have changed," one of them remarked wisely. Youth, however, would have none of it; they were determined to reassert old Rajput dominance and to do it as they had always done it in the past, by dividing the Vankars.

In all the above happenings the leading role had been played by the younger Vankars. The Rajputs taunted the Vankar elders: "You have lost your authority. You have ceased to be the leaders of your community." Their strategy worked. Three of the elders took the side of the Rajputs. With a divided community and with two different cases going on, the Vankars were now on the defensive. The *mahetars* advised the cooperative to withdraw the case and accept a verbal assurance from the Rajputs that no further damage would be done. The cooperative case was withdrawn, Vankar unity restored.

In the new climate of reconciliation and, at the request of both the MLA and the Bhal's Rajput leader, the Vankars agreed to withdraw the case of rape. However, that was no longer possible since it had become a government case, and government alone could withdraw it. The solution suggested by the Rajputs and, in all innocence, accepted by the Vankars was to submit contradictory testimony so that the case would not stand. As luck would have it, the magistrate in Cambay was a Vankar himself who challenged the new witnesses and cross-examined them until they confessed to their perjury. The whole incident was noted down by the understanding magistrate as further proof of Rajput harassment and interference with the process of law. The case is still pending.

Except for these repeated skirmishes, the relations between Rajputs and Vankars never went out of control. The real fight with the Rajputs was to be fought not in Pandad but in Golana; and it was again the younger group, not the elders, who played a crucial role.

Golana, 1984. The cooperative movement was five years old in the Bhal. The former barren fields of Vadgam now looked green and lush, a treat to man and beast alike. This example had already impressed Gudel and Pandad, and now Valli, Vainej and Mithli were ready to join. Government had given facilities in Daheda. If the Rajputs in Golana did not rise to the occasion, their village would soon have an efficient Vankar cooperative. The Golana Rajputs felt that they had to make a stand and reverse this trend with cunning, if possible; by force, if necessary.

They had used force effectively in the past. Three years after the very first course was given to a group of Vankars of this village, the Centre received an urgent message from Golana, "Please, come here immediately." That was in 1978. When the Centre's senior men arrived, there was a hushed silence in the Vankar neighbourhood. Nobody dared raise his voice. One of the young leaders had beaten a Rajput who had had an affair with a Vankar woman. Similar cases had happened in the past, but this time, some mischievous Vankars shamed the father of the young Rajput in public by telling him of both his son's misbehaviour and of his consequent punishment. For the father it was now a question of prestige. He made it known that he would kill the Vankar who had beaten his son. The people were afraid. The Centre's men were asked," What will the Centre do if one of us is murdered? Will the Centre make sure that criminal proceedings are started immediately? On the Centre's assurances, their fears subsided. Many people claimed, however, that the first casualty had already taken place. The brother of the threatened young man had died a few days earlier. Fear killed him, they thought.

When the Rajputs came to know of the Centre's promise, they quietly let it be known that for the time being nothing would happen: "Let these Ahmedabad people withdraw, and then we shall see."

Six years later, knowing for sure that the Centre was there to stay, the Rajputs changed their strategy from threats to bribes, in an effort to keep some of the traditional leaders away from the cooperative. Their efforts succeeded during 1984; a number of factors came to their help.

First, the Centre's performance during 1984 was not very good. Although the cooperative had not yet started officially, the Centre had agreed to start working in some of the fields. Its first efforts at conventional agriculture were not very successful. To cap it all, part of the would-be cooperative's fields were wiped out by the river which, as a result of a flood, changed course. The Rajputs added to these miseries by turning their cattle loose in the only flourishing field of the would-be cooperative and thus ruining it. The Centre was not quick enough to complain and ask for compensation.

Second, among the Vankars, there was competition between the Hindu and Christian leaders. Catholic priests, it has been mentioned earlier, had been working in this area and had converted to Christianity about 10 per cent of the Vankars in this village. The most intelligent and dedicated educational worker the Centre had in the Bhal was from Golana and was a Christian, Paul. Another young man, Pochabhai had inherited the traditional leadership and become one of the *mahetars* in Golana. As long as Gaga Natha was alive, Pochabhai was forced to play second fiddle. But after Gaga Natha's death Pochabhai, young, farsighted and hard-driving had gained prominence – to the alarm of the older *mahetars* who wanted to step into Gaga Natha's shoes. The Rajputs could easily play one set of *mahetars* against the other. Indeed, they could easily arouse Hindu fears of Christian domination in the cooperative which, the Rajputs asserted, would certainly be run by Pochabhai and Paul!

The balance began to shift in favour of the cooperative in 1985. By then Paul's persistence and Pochabhai's magnanimity won over virtually all the leaders and their followers except Vithal, who had always been a puppet of the Rajputs. It was now up to the meeting of all the *mahetars* to decide the course of action. Vithal was thrown out of the *jati* together with his followers. No official members of the

Vankar *jati* remained opposed to the cooperative. The elders could truthfully give the Centre the good news: "*All* the Vankars are ready to join the cooperative." Of course, the elders' action was symbolic. It was meant to tell Vithal that his divisive action would not be tolerated and that he and his followers would have to face social ostracism. Sooner or later, everybody knew, they would return to the fold and would then join the cooperative.

Bribes and cunning having failed, the Rajputs now decided to use force. Rumours soon spread in the village that Bhupatsingh (pseudonym) had gathered a group of Rajputs in their temple. It was not clear what happened there; but, it was said, an oath had been taken to kill Pochabhai, Paul and other cooperative officials. The Vankars decided that Paul would not go to his fields, since he could easily be murdered there. Pochabhai would take care never to go alone. A surprise attack in a solitary place without witnesses to testify later was the people's main fear.

The decisive issue in the Vankar-Rajput war was a housing society. Under a government scheme, scheduled castes were eligible for grants of both land and money to build their houses. The Vankars applied for and were granted an ideal plot of land close to their present houses and the village pond. The ground was strategically important in the present caste war. Granting it to the Vankars was, therefore, totally unacceptable to the Rajputs who fought tooth and nail to have the plot taken away from them. They approached the bureaucracy. The local MLA was asked to exert pressure on the district and taluka administration. It was all in vain. The Rajputs then hired a lawyer who had a 'stay order' issued to the revenue department (forbidding the revenue department to make any further grants until the case was heard).

It was not meant for the Vankars. Still the Rajput lawyer used that document to stop the Vankars from working on the site. The Centre's lawyer appealed to the magistrate who issued a stern warning to the Rajput lawyer. It was now quite clear to the Rajputs that their case was lost. They had to act quickly. Physical punishment alone would teach the Vankars a lesson they would never forget.

The Rajputs sought allies in their war. They persuaded the other scheduled castes – a small group of Bhangis and Rohits – "Your houses should also be built along with those of the Vankars. It is your right. If you fight for it, you will get it. Tomorrow when the

Vankars go there to work, you, too, go and fight against them. We shall help you."

The judgement of the Session Court in its typical, dry, legal language explains what happened subsequently (pp. 3-5):

"On 25-1-86 at about 8-00 A.M. the accused Gafurbhai, Govindbhai Jethabhai and Atabhai had gone to this land. They had carried with them wooden poles etc. They had started digging for the purpose of erecting [. . .] huts. Complainant Pochabhai Kalabhai and others came to know about this and so they went to the spot. They had tried to persuade them not to assume possession of the land and to desist from making unauthorised construction therein. It is alleged that the above persons got excited at that time and that accused Gafurbhai aimed a dharia at Itchabhai Lalabhai. [. . .]

Thereafter the complainant and others decided to go to Khambhat police station for the purpose of filing complaint. [. . .] So they all came to the bus-stand of their village. They found one truck in a stationary condition at that place. They talked to the driver. Rs. 100 were fixed as travelling charges. Thereafter they all set in that truck. [. . .] at that point of time many persons armed with different weapons [. . .] came from the side of Rajputwas [. . .] They all were raising shouts that they be killed there and then. [. . .] The persons of the mob surrounded the truck. They had tried to drag out Khodabhai, Lalabhai and Ranchodbhai from the driver's cabin. They also started beating them. Therefore, those persons of the Vankar community sitting in the rear body of the truck jumped out and started running towards their locality. They were chased. Some of them were injured. They all came running in their maholla [locality]. This took place at about 9-30 A.M.

It is alleged that sometime thereafter a mob consisting of many persons armed with different weapons such as guns, dharias, sticks, kodalis, dantis, etc, came from the side of the Rajputwas. [. . .] Gun shots were fired. Therefore, the persons belonging to Vankar community took to their heels. Some concealed themselves in their own houses. Some concealed themselves in the houses of others. Some ran away to distant places. The persons in the mob tried to break open the doors of some houses for the purpose of forcing their entry therein. [. . .] Some persons were seriously injured. Prabhubhai Pochabhai was chased and the accused Chandubhai, Jamubhai and Natubhai had fired at him. He had received gun shot injuries. He was bodily lifted and taken by some of the accused to the inner part of the house of Dahyabhai Mulabhai where he was again fired at, with the result that he died there. Pochabhai Punjabhai managed to run away from his house. However, he was also followed and ultimately he was also shot at, with the result that he died of gun shot injuries. Mohanbhai Mithabhai and Khodabhai Mithabhai also sustained serious injuries which ultimately resulted in their deaths."

It was the 25th of January, 1986, the eve of Republic Day which commemorates the coming into effect of the new Constitution, which, ironically, had made untouchability a cognisable offence. Blood, consternation and silent tears were all that Golana could offer to celebrate Republic Day, 1986. When the Chief Minister of Gujarat visited Golana, he was greeted by a Vankar leader's agonising cry: "Sir, do we have a right to live in this country?"

As the sun set on that fateful day, four corpses were brought from the Cambay and Ahmedabad hospitals, received amid the hardly contained cries of grief of close relatives and the silent tears of the Vankars from Golana and neighbouring villages. Fear had given way to dignity: they had been left alone to grieve over their dead.

The scheduled castes bury their own secretly. Living with dignity, dying with honour, these four symbols of an awakened consciousness and a regained self-worth, deserved better. They were buried in the middle of the planned housing society, in the presence of all their brethren, press reporters, politicians, religious leaders and the grieving members of the Centre. Their tombs are adorned with flowers. Visited by Vankars from far and near, the tombs are sometimes kept aglow with lighted candles proclaiming in death what these men had always fought for in life, self-respect and the affirmation of human dignity.

To spread panic, to cause helplessness and to have the Vankars return to slavish dependence had been the goals of the Rajput attack. And that was indeed the initial reaction. But, not for long. That funeral, the daily peregrination of Vankars from all over Gujarat silently leaving their donations at the feet of the *mahetars*, the uninterrupted presence of the Centre, the visits of political parties, voluntary organisations, private individuals and even a Minister from the central government (a Gujarati Vankar himself), all had their impact on the people.

Outside reaction had been expected by the assailants – that was why they fled. But they also expected that the outsiders would soon leave and forget, that they would contrive to elude justice and return to the village to terrorise their victims. A fair trial was essential to frustrate their designs. The police had to act honestly and competently. Golana needed legal advice and a constant follow-up to prevent the unscrupulous use of money or political pressure. Somebody would have to coordinate all these efforts.

The *nat* (assembly of all village elders) met after the completion of the official mourning period and their funeral customs. In this meeting all the *mahetars* of the Bhal called on the Centre to follow up the Golana case. As the Centre took up this task, an enlightened bureaucrat remarked, "This massacre may either catapult the Vankars into the 21st century or back into the Middle Ages. Much will depend on you, gentlemen."

A reputed firm of lawyers was hired (they refused to accept any remuneration). Their first concern was to have a good criminal lawyer appointed public prosecutor. The Chief Minister had agreed to have a special prosecutor for this case and promised to have the *nat* representatives' choice nominated. The police, meanwhile, had acted swiftly and competently: within 10 days 31 persons were behind bars, among them the main suspects. Fear of outside interference in the preparation of the police case was always present and the Vankar community exerted its own political influence to counteract such interference. In early 1987 the case came up for hearing at the Nadiad Sessions Court. On the 12th of June, 14 people were sentenced to life imprisonment. Efforts either to divide the Vankar community or to intimidate the witnesses had failed. On the witness stand, it was perhaps the women who made the greatest impact. Be that as it may, the fact that the whole community stood united and firm, and, as a result, the fact that murder did not go unpunished, restored both self-respect and faith in democracy to the Vankar community, not only in Golana but in the whole Bhal.

The local administration, having failed to stop the massacre, tried to make up for this failure with generous grants. The cooperative movement caught their eye. Large subsidies were sanctioned to finance the afforestation work (see Table 8) and a housing complex at Golana which turned out to be an example of local involvement and people's initiative. As a result, government's money stretched itself out to build houses double the size of others in similar schemes. Delighted at the efficiency of the work, Delhi officials sanctioned an additional grant for a community hall. This is government's way of telling the high castes that their murderous designs will not pay.

The Golana incident is a sad witness to the radical nature of the cooperative movement. The Rajputs were not moved to violence for economic reasons, although these could not be ignored. More than the economic losses, they feared that caste privileges were slipping away from them. They dreaded facing the fact that those whom they despised were claiming rights.

The sad reality is that caste people (i.e. those who really *belong* to the caste system) refuse to accept the existence of the former outcastes. Of course, they do accept it just as we accept the existence of disease: something to get rid of, if possible, to be endured, otherwise. The very first aim, therefore, of the cooperative movement had been to assert that the former outcastes did exist. Existence entails rights: they should have equal rights.

From Caste to Class

For all its oppression, the caste system is only *one* of the ways in which people are divided. There are other divisions: the rich versus the poor, the urban versus the rural, the educated versus the illiterate and, most important of all, those who have political power against the rest. Most rural people in the Bhal are poor. Ironically, now that the cooperatives give employment to the Vankars, even high caste people are worse off than the former outcastes. The time has come for the Vankar *jati* to do for the other *jatis* what urban people have been doing for them during the last ten years. The point needs some elaboration.

Long-range development ultimately rests on the ability of people to influence government, that is, on building up political power. Government is the repository of the state's resources. Government through the use of punishments and rewards can *coerce* people. When this is done to uphold the privileges of some to the detriment of others, government is friendly with the former and hostile to the latter. Government defends injustice and exploitation. The rule of law presupposes that all citizens have equal rights and that the state guarantees those rights. In practice, however, "eternal vigilance" is required to defend one's rights. It is not enough to make sure that a government is not hostile; poor people need a positively friendly government which will allow them to share in the national wealth in spite of their social, economic, educational and other handicaps. Over a period of time this requires political leverage. Do the scheduled castes have this political power? The previous narration suggests that they do. Public opinion feels guilty about the practice of untouchability. Fair people do not grudge but, rather, welcome affirmative action. But this cannot last for ever. There will be a backlash – or, can it be avoided?

To begin with, the scheduled castes are about 100 million (Joshi, 1986: 50) out of India's total population of 750 million i.e., approximately 13 per cent (14.6 per cent according to the 1971 census). In absolute numbers they are many, but relatively speaking, they are a small minority of the population. In Gujarat they are only 6.8 per cent of the population.

It is the majority which rules in a democracy; this means that in India caste people (as opposed to the outcastes) govern the nation. In other words, the scheduled castes do not have enough political power unless they federate with other *jatis*. Translated to the Bhal situation, this means that the Vankars' achievements can easily be swept away unless they win over the cooperation of other *jatis*.

Several factors should make this cooperation easy in spite of caste prejudices. First, there are many educated Vankars who can play a very positive role in any developmental work. Second, they are now efficiently running cooperatives which have been able to mobilise substantial financial resources and government subsidies. Third, they have created and maintained a healthy relationship with the Centre, an urban group, which can similarly help other deserving *jatis*.

A federation of castes as a political strategy has been adopted by other castes in India (Rudolph, 1966; Kothari, 1970). Within Gujarat, a number of lower castes have grouped themselves with the high caste Rajputs under the name of Kshatriyas (Kothari, Maru, 1970) to gain political power. The need for a broad-based federation of marginalised groups has been proclaimed by many people. Even the Congress party's strategy in Gujarat advocated the alliance of the Kshatriyas, Harijans, Adivasis (tribals) and Muslims – the so called KHAM strategy. Unfortunately, much faith cannot be placed in such strategies which depend on the political mood of the moment. More hopefully, groups of scheduled castes themselves have seen the need. Barbara Joshi (1986:108) describes the best known among them:

Beginning in the 1970s, one association begun by Dalit government employees, BAMCEF, constructed a multistate base, a chain of journals printed in several different languages, and an ideology that emphasized cooperation among Dalits (scheduled castes), tribals, religious minorities and low status Hindu castes. Members come from a variety of these groups, and have jobs that range from peon to skilled technician to administrator. Organisation style has emphasized identification with the poor rather than middle-class display.

This organisation has its branches in Gujarat and some educated Vankars have joined its ranks. Unfortunately, they have not been able to catch the imagination of the electorate and, so far, have done poorly at the polls. Serious political work demands slow and patient spadework at the grassroots. People have very concrete needs which demand immediate attention. Structures which take care of these needs win the confidence of the people. The cooperative movement does precisely that. If this movement in the Bhal rises to the occasion and comes to the help of other *jatis*, then it will become a socio-economic force in the area and its political survival will be guaranteed.

Summary

To sum up, the success of the cooperative movement in the Bhal will ultimately depend on its ability to relate meaningfully to all the other *jatis*. As economic self-sufficiency frees the Vankars from socio-economic bondage, and as their organisational power and the underlying technical and managerial expertise qualify them to carry out tasks which negate their former status of untouchables, they can now relate to other *jatis* in a manner which will also negate caste ideology. First, because organisational ability and economic self-reliance make meaningful political participation possible. Secondly, because such qualification enhances their stature and, consequently, their social standing. Thirdly, because this expertise enables the lower castes to help the higher castes. This may be the equaliser required to lay the foundation of a caste federation and, eventually, a class formation.

The policy, so far, has been to accept the *jati* as a *Gemeinschaft* which it surely is, while at the same time moving towards a

Gesellschaft, trying to preserve the best of both. The aim is the creation or preservation of intermediate groups as an antidote against the excessive *atomisation* of society. The strong sense of self-identity, the deeply satisfying human relationships possible in a community are psychological reasons in its favour. Politically, too, intermediate groups are a check on the excessive power of the state. They facilitate the articulation of interests and can control the selfishness of individuals.

Admittedly, the abolition of all *jati* groups, say by intercaste marriages, would exorcise caste ideology more effectively. The Centre's aim, however, is not a negative one, the mere abolition, of caste ideology, but a positive one, the creation of self-managed, financially self-sufficient, socially viable communities of humanised persons.

The Centre, choosing to work within the *jati* groups, distances itself from most radical revolutionary movements. It (1) rejects caste ideology, (2) works with the more marginalised groups, and (3) insists on cooperative production rather than private enterprise and private property, thus setting itself apart from conservative and liberal individualism. This is an important topic which will be taken up later.

The Cooperatives and the Centre

By 1977 the activities of the Centre had won the confidence of some funding agencies which volunteered to finance so that the centre could pay professional salaries to its staff. It then became necessary to set up a separate trust. It was officially registered as *The St. Xavier's Nonformal Education Society*. The Jesuit Province of Gujarat assumed the legal responsibility for the new trust and society. The provincial superior of the Jesuits became the president of the new society's governing body, the principal of St. Xavier's College, its vice-president and the director of the Centre its secretary. All these were Jesuit priests. The senior-most persons in the Centre, a Parsi and a Muslim, were nominated to the board of trustees.

The core group of the Centre was the Educational Wing. Initially two, later three, and ultimately five persons made up this wing. The Educational Wing has seen a high number of staff leaving the Centre, from its very inception. Fortunately, the Centre's own post-graduate fellowship programme has been a fertile recruiting ground: of the present staff of five only one is not an FPSM alumnus.

A Technical Wing was set up in 1980. The need for technical personnel became evident the moment the Centre decided to manage agricultural cooperatives. Later, this technical expertise was utilised to help other tribal cooperatives which were not managed by the Centre (see Appendix 2). The Technical Wing initially had an agriculture graduate from Gujarat University. Soon two young recruits from the Indian Institute of Management joined. One had an agriculture degree, the other had one in veterinary science. They have trained their own staff in agriculture and animal husbandry. Later, two more persons joined them: one in charge of the administrative services and the other with a post-graduate diploma in forestry. The technical wing covers all the technical and managerial tasks which running a cooperative entails. It also explains to the people what is being done and the scientific principles required to understand it.

The Educational Wing had the final say in all matters which were not exclusively technical. This right was an assertion of man over technology and of people over projects.

In 1984 the Centre set up a Post-graduate training and research centre manned by professors from the college working on a part-time basis. The aim of this programme was to train people to work for development.

The Centre and the Cooperatives

As a development worker, one is often asked by well-meaning, educated, urban friends, "You are surely doing excellent work. But, now, tell me. When are you going to hand over all responsibilities to the local people?" The local people, on the other hand, ask another question, "Are you going to remain with us or are you going to leave us like most people in the past?" What is the relationship between the 'insider' and the 'outsider'?

The Centre had stated its position in 1981 (1981 Annual Report):

A key question in development is: What is the role of the 'outsider'? Does he take the initiative at the risk of pushing the local community to the back seat or does he sit back until they take the initiative?

The Centre's initial answer was to sit back, educate and wait for them to act. Previous reports have shown how the Centre moved into active involvement, seen as an integral part of its educational work.

The same report proposed three steps to make sure that the local community retained the initiative:

First: To explain clearly to all the cooperators the Centre's position and to act always according to that position which was stated as follows:

1. *Ownership* of the cooperative assets as well as *control* over the new inputs (financial, technological and managerial) is in the hands of the local community. The Centre acts as manager.

2. The owners are the masters and therefore control the managers.

3. Matters of policy are decided by the owners or their appointed Executive Committee.

4. The role of the manager is to apprise the owners of the technical problems and their various solutions.

5. The day-to-day administration of the cooperative will initially be in the hands of the managers until gradually the Executive Committee can take over.

6. Individual benefits will be decided by the owners.

7. All money transactions and accounts are handled by the managers; accounts are to be submitted regularly at the general meetings.

This last clause was subsequently changed to read, "accounts are maintained at Daheda by the office of the proposed federation." Accounts of the closing and the budget for the opening month are submitted by the technical personnel of the cooperative to its finance committee.

8. Agricultural experimentation is in the hands of the Centre's agricultural manager until local talent can take it over. Marketing also remains in his hands.

Second: To select a few local individuals for full-time specialised training. Since that meant giving up their usual source of income, a monthly stipend was agreed upon.

Third: To start the process of withdrawal very gradually but at an early stage.

Important though the above understanding between the Centre and the cooperatives may be, it does not portray even faintly the relationship which has been established between the two. The relationship is founded on inner attitudes which have developed over years. To understand these, one could perhaps study the motivation which develops in the Centre's staff as they work with the rural poor. An in-depth study would be fascinating but not feasible at this moment. On the other hand, without analysing their motivation, it will not be easy to understand how they relate to the people they work with. This inner attitude of the Centre's personnel may perhaps be understood by studying the needs which are satisfied in the Centre.

The need for meaning. In a country with 250 million people living below the poverty line, an effort to forego urban comforts and to work for the poor is not only a generous gesture but one which makes sense, all the more if action for the poor is preceded by planning based on serious study of the root causes of poverty and is followed by a ruthless evaluation. As problems and difficulties are studied and solved, a legitimate pride is experienced which, subsequently, becomes a driving force in maintaining high standards. It is not so much that one can raise an accusing finger at uncaring citizens, not even that one can find fault with other agencies doing more amateurish work, but the satisfaction, the inner happiness, of doing something meaningful and doing it well. Any group, all the more one which runs counter to accepted norms and values, must justify its existence in terms of ends and means which make sense. This the Centre does.

Job satisfaction. Apart from the satisfaction of working for the downtrodden just mentioned, the day-to-day work has its share of joys – pain, frustration and discouragement notwithstanding. This joy springs from two different sources: one is the joy of learning how to deal with village groups effectively and the other is the relationship with the villagers which results. True to its earlier skills in the behavioural sciences, the Centre's team has developed keen observation powers; the ability to find the real issue in the plethora of verbal decoys and diversionary tactics of village culture; and the skill to recognise and accept feelings, gently laying aside more cerebral and less relevant issues. The result is communication. Feelings recognised and accepted stop frustrating games, pull down barriers of inequality or cultural differences or conflicting interests and open up the gates of communication. This has been the Centre's greatest asset. When dialogue takes place, common understanding is possible and creative solutions are already in the making. Incubation periods can, of course, be frustratingly long. Life moves much faster in the cities than in the villages. Some people are quicker at grasping things than others. Consequently the pace at which people move is different. The Centre accepts the pace at which the other moves.

Symbols help communication, and the Centre makes use of them: insistence on sitting on the ground like everybody else; refusal to be addressed as "sahib"; use of respectful words while conversing with the people; deliberate disregard of caste rules which prevent members of a higher caste from dining with those of the scheduled castes.

More important, the Centre has acquired over the years a fund of knowledge and experience in dealing with the Vankars and their traditional leaders which greatly facilitates its work today. Many years of association create a bond of unity and affection which is very similar to that existing within the Centre's staff. That is why, as mentioned earlier, affiliation needs are satisfied in the work itself. Indeed, the identification is almost complete. Any mismanagement in the cooperatives is seen as a reflection on the Centre's competence and, conversely, their progress is seen as an indication of its success.

There is something beautiful in this and something dangerous, too. Identification with sectoral interests, when stretched too far, may work against the common good and ultimately become self-defeating. A less distant danger is that of strengthening casteism and delaying a class formation based on the unity of *all* the poor.

The Centre is aware of these and is ready to take steps to guard against them.

The Centre is aware of other dangers, as well. Its very organisation has some internal contradictions which may hamper its work. The fact that it has various units (see Table 12) may lead to friction. Its very hierarchical organisation, and the fact that there are four different grades with different pay scales (the highest receives a salary four times the salary of the lowest) may militate against the very equality it advocates. The initial ethos of the Centre did emphasise equality. Decisions were arrived at by consensus, individuals were encouraged to air their views. Open criticism was encouraged. But as the group grew, the structures within the Centre itself weighed more heavily, the initial informality has given way to a more formal managerial system. Like any other human institution, the Centre has its shortcomings and limitations. The question is, will these prevent it from realising the vision which it has?

Table 12 : **Organisation of the Behavioural Science Centre**

Director			
Research & Formal Education	Educational Wing	Technical Wing	Administration
Dean & Research Associate	2 Sr officers 1 Jr officer	Agriculture Manager Vet.Doctor & assistants	Accountant, Assistant & attendants

Social awareness can help to rise above institutional constraints. There is also a need to rise above one's own activities. The research section is meant to help the activists in their process of reflection. A man removed from the place of action has a more detached view of things. Detachment is required to gain objectivity. Here the research scholars can help, as they perform two other tasks. First, they keep the educational and technical wings posted on activist and development literature. There are many people all over the world working for development and they carry out many interesting experiments. Their knowledge and experience may be invaluable to avoid costly mistakes. They may also provide ideas to improve the Centre's development work.

The second task is to help the Centre carry out a good, scientific evaluation of the work already done. Scientific evaluation is a sure means to improving one's own performance.

However, the most immediate step contemplated by the Centre and all the cooperatives to achieve this autonomy is the establishment of a federation. According to present state legislation, a federation is composed of at least six cooperatives desirous to federate and one or two outside agencies willing and able to help. Daheda has been chosen as an ideal place for the federation head-quarters, as explained earlier, with some facilities already built up: a warehouse, offices, living quarters and a place where training sessions can be conducted. It has 50 acres of land on which experimentation in forestry is being conducted. When the federation is formally set up, government may be able to allot more land. There are plenty of wastelands in this place.

The federation should take up all the managerial, technical and administrative tasks at present carried out by the Centre. It will own equipment which can be used by each member cooperative without its having to be duplicated in purchase. All the purchases and sales of the cooperatives will be centralised at Daheda to obtain better prices and to lower the overheads.

Each cooperative and the Centre will have one representative each on the board of the federation. The administrative set-up is now being studied. The draft proposal will be studied by all the cooperatives, their comments taken into consideration, and the final draft approved by them will be submitted to government together with all the papers required to have the federation registered. We expect this to take place soon.

Returning to the question of power (the Centre vs. the cooperatives) in the federation. The Centre will not have voting power – all powers will be vested with the federating units. In another sense, they have always been powerful, because dialogue has been the cornerstone in the dealings of the Centre with the Vankars. When their interests are at stake and the Centre has ignored them, they have always argued their case with fierce conviction. In such circumstances, manipulation is not possible.

The Centre still plays a crucial role. It must help the cooperatives to make the long-range vision of the Centre their own: to make sure that *jati* groups do not become selfishly exclusive. Their group identity as Vankars should not prevent them from making the cooperative movement help other groups. Unity strengthened by cooperation can turn all these groups into a political force. This the Centre must do. Its moral authority and its fund of goodwill must be used to convey this vision in a convincing manner.

7

SUMMARY AND CONCLUSIONS: THE MEANING OF DEVELOPMENT

This study is one of the many manifestations of man's restlessness and his desire to improve things. The work described above was carried out by educators. Their professional bias is, therefore, likely to colour the whole analysis.

Development presupposes a movement from something less good to something better. This, of course, must be based on value judgments. And values need not be accepted universally. In fairness to our readers, these values should now be clearly stated.

This study presupposes that a person is a *relational* being. He relates to himself, since he is constantly in dialogue with himself. Fear of his true self prevents a person from facing himself: noise, constant occupation, entertainments, social engagements are some of the many ways in which man drowns this fear and runs away from his deepest self – personal alienation. This study presupposes that a person grows and develops mainly from within. The more a person is in touch with himself, the greater his power and mastery. The more one stays with one's own feelings, the greater one's *awareness*. Of course, other human beings can help one master one's fears and heighten one's awareness. But, ultimately, a person must face himself, for the greatest battles of the world are fought in the loneliness of one's own heart. In this solitude and silence poor mortals may experience the Transcendent.

A person's ability to relate to himself determines his ability to relate to others. The relational nature of human beings finds expression in their sociability. Social intercourse, this study assumes, is meant to enrich oneself and others. Whatever fosters such enrichment is *functional*, what prevents it is *dysfunctional*. Conflict, if properly dealt with, far from being dysfunctional can lead to growth and development.

Social relations are seldom free of pressures arising from the economic conditions prevailing in society. These conditions or "socio-economic structures" must be closely monitored if individual freedom is to be preserved. The old adage, "Eternal vigilance is the price of freedom" has found a new expression in "Social awareness leads to liberation",an awareness which often entails a political fight.

Development, this study assumes, is an attempt to create a society in which exploitation is not possible. This, of course, means the creation of new social, economic and political structures. The aim may be utopian. The attempt is not. It may be utopian to think that a society can be established in which exploitation is not possible. But it is not impossible to make the attempt. It should be done: the dialectical relationship between the reality of evil and the possibility of good leads to moral progress and prevents society from sliding down the path of amorality and unredeemed selfishness.

Few individuals and fewer groups give up privilege willingly. That is why the fight against exploitation has to be waged by *empowering* the weak. This is precisely what this book narrates: the efforts of several educators to empower one of the weakest sections of Indian society, the former untouchables. To empower a weak group means:
1. To help the group achieve that *social awareness* which makes each individual realise how society conditions him/her. More specifically the manner in which:

  a. the powerful *divide* the poor the better to rule over them;

  b. the powerful *despise* the weak and design ideologies to prove that the poor deserve nothing but contempt;

  c. the powerful keep the poor *ignorant* the better to control them;

  d. the powerful keep them *economically dependent* as the most effective means to enrich themselves and to prevent the poor from fighting for their rights.

Awareness among the oppressed leads to their realisation of their need for: first, *unity*, second, restoring their *self-respect*; third, *education*; and, finally, expression of their unity in *cooperative enterprises* as the best means to offset the economic power of the rich.

2. The development of their *organisational ability* in an economic enterprise, this study asserts, must go hand in hand with the effort to raise the group's social awareness.

The peculiar social conditions of the scheduled castes in India demand that they set up separate economic organisations until they can relate to the higher castes on a footing of equality. Their new skills and their newly gained economic self-sufficiency should help the former untouchables to be socially accepted by the others.

3. The creation of *intermediate, self-managed* groups is the immediate aim of the Centre's efforts: neither Soviet *etatism* nor unbridled liberal individualism leading to an *atomised* society are seen as models which can prevent exploitation. This study postulates the need for smaller, intermediate groups in which individuals can preserve a strong sense of belonging and identity. The state therefore should be "one nation made up of self-managed groups where every individual counts, where the masses are empowered and, consequently, democracy is not a myth – a cover for the dictatorship of vested interests – but a reality" (1983 Annual Report).

4. The *autonomy* of these intermediate groups requires that (1) they become economically *self-sufficient*, (2) their members maintain a high degree of *social awareness*, and (3) the community as a whole imbibe a minimum amount of scientific or *technological knowledge* to compete effectively with similar groups within and outside the country.

The Centre's approach to rural development is both radical and conservative. It is radical in that it seeks significant changes in the existing socio-economic structures. But it is not radical in the sense used by those thinkers who advocate a revolution which does away with *all* existing structures and replaces them with new ones. Such a task can be accomplished by the state alone. Logically, these thinkers do *not* want intermediate groups which would take power away from the state or obstruct their revolution. While some of these revolutions have made impressive gains initially, later, they have reached a point of stagnation and rigidity which has prevented normal growth.

Apart from these ideological considerations, there is no doubt that the educational profession of the Centre's staff was an important factor in the Centre's decision to shun political activism. The 1983 Report stated the Centre's position:

The Centre questions the meaning of revolution. A revolution is good if it gives power to the people. [To achieve this, much] work has to be done [with the people] either before or during the revolution. Else, after the revolution power will continue to be in the hands of the few, the new elites.

. . .governments are always the reflection of society. If society is divided between those who know and those who do not, government will also reflect that division and, no matter who wields power, such a division will create an exploitative situation.

Therefore, to delay the transfer of technology until the revolution takes place is not only unwise but contrary to the avowed principles of true revolutionaries.

It is true that in this process of development there is danger of compromises, of maintaining the status quo and even of being manipulated by vested interests to retard rather than to foster a true revolution.

To ward off these dangers there is need, on the part of the outsiders, of a true commitment to the people, and, on the part of all, of an understanding of society both as it is and as it should be.

This does not mean that the Centre does not realise the importance of political activity. On the contrary, it believes that a community comes really into its own only when it can take meaningful part in the political life of the nation. Much of the training the Centre imparts aims precisely at raising social and political awareness. The organisational ability acquired by the people in running a cooperative, together with the resulting self-sufficiency form the best foundation on which a solid political future can be built.

But the Centre is equally clear on another point: the people themselves should decide their course of political action.

The Centre's Pedagogy

The Centre's pedagogy is naturally based on its philosophy. Thus, for example, since feelings are considered an important component of human nature, they are made to play an important role in the Centre's educational programme. There are three different stages in this educational process:

First stage: Group training leading to social awareness.
Second stage: Social awareness leading to group action. The scheduled caste sets up its own cooperative.
Third stage: "Education" in and through the cooperative.

1. *Group training*. The goal of this training is to counteract the harmful effects which unjust socio-economic structures and their ideology have had on the subjectivity of each individual and on the group as a whole. Caste ideology in India tames the people into subjection, as explained in detail in Appendix 1, which also highlights the importance of the unconscious in ideological formation.

The harmful effects mentioned earlier (loss of self-respect, factional fights, overdependence, ignorance), must be opposed first at the *unconscious* level. This is done through the use of symbols, fantasy, and the experience of the feelings generated during the training sessions. Finally the lived experience of unity and mutual support within the group is a lesson by itself. The aim is to have *self-respect* accepted as the most important value in the new culture which the group evolves during the course, hoping that this value will be carried along to the situation back home.

The group is also encouraged to share its concerns. Indeed, oppressive concerns must be made to surface and be faced squarely. Otherwise they burden the unconscious and prevent *creativity*. A burden is oppressive when it is carried by a single individual, but a shared burden becomes lighter. Again, the certainty of the group's support removes the greatest of fears, that of not being accepted by one's own brethren. When fear vanishes, the creative power of men is unleashed.

The *critical awareness* of the group is raised by having the participants reflect on the socio-economic structures of their own village, on the origin of their knowledge, on the purpose of the ideological myths prevalent in society, on their own factional fights (who benefits and who suffers under them), on their economic dependence and the means to achieve self-sufficiency.

Practical skills in self-expression or the ability to communicate with others, conflict resolution, planning, decision-making, dealing with the bureaucracy, etc., are also imparted when the group is faced with issues which demand such skills.

2. *Group action.* Action is seen as part of the whole educational process. Indeed, the very aim of group training is action in the village which is planned during the training itself. The action usually requires a number of meetings with the elders and the representatives of all the households to arrive at a consensus on the establishment of a cooperative. It also requires that each household be convinced to buy shares, as necessary qualification for cooperative membership. It entails having the cooperative registered with the civil authorities and deciding on the composition of the executive committee and the election of its chairman. It may mean applying to government for the land required and other facilities to which a cooperative for the scheduled castes is entitled.

The dynamics within the meetings held to arrive at concerted action present important learning situations which help the group grow in self-understanding. Some of its members are helped to deal with their own limitations, their dysfunctional behaviour, and to refine their skills in dealing with other individuals and the group.

3. *The cooperative as a university.* The cooperative is two things: first, a radical change in the economic structures which give rise to a new set of social relations. Second, as a result of that, the cooperative is a school in which new learning can take place on technological, managerial, social, and political issues, as occasion demands.

The educator, we have repeatedly asserted, cannot remain in an aseptic world, far removed from the daily striving, the successes and failures, of human effort. Learning is a slow, painful process of involvement in the life of the people and in the production process itself. Without thus learning, teaching is not possible, be it in social structures or in technology.

The cooperative offers a unique structure from which the main obstacles to learning have been removed: there is no dichotomy between the teacher and the taught because in the cooperative everybody learns and everybody teaches as the problems of production, labour or management are faced by all together. The subject matter is not irrelevant; because it deals with the problems the people face here and now. The learning and, therefore, the knowledge acquired is not alienating nor does it lead to a fragmented existence (knowing more and more about less and less) because it deals with every aspect of the people's lives.

The cooperative is an economic unit in which the community owns and controls the means of production. It is also a socio-cultural community where all the individuals relate to one another as human beings, brothers of a family. It is also a political community which fights for its rights. It has no place for either inane intellectualism or shallow activism. The life of the poor is a struggle for survival and against exploitation. It is not an academic exercise.

An agricultural cooperative in which experts and ordinary farmers work together is a place where *transfer of technology* in the best sense of the word can take place. Ordinary activism focuses too much on economic inequalities. Not that they are unimportant. But they are only part of a more complex reality. *Knowledge* is as good a commodity as land or ready cash, maybe better.

No community can claim equality with the rest of society as long as it lags way behind others in scientific or technological knowledge. Deprived of access to the ever-increasing fund of scientific knowledge and to the manner of applying it to concrete circumstances, such a community cannot make the best of available resources. It is at a disadvantage. And this, being a continuous process, keeps distancing such a community more and more from those that are better educated. An effective transfer of technology alone can reverse this trend.

Transfer of technology presupposes two things: first a thorough understanding of the local circumstances and, second, mastery of the technology to be transferred. 'Foreign' experts often fail in the first and the local population in the second condition. A technology which is not understood by those using it can hardly be said to have been transferred. That is clear. But there is more to it. In agriculture, at least, knowledge of the land, the local weather, and understanding of the people and their condition all have to be taken into consideration when new agricultural practices are introduced. What has been successful in one place may not be equally successful in another when the experiment is replicated elsewhere. Replication seldom works. Local conditions may demand small but important changes.

The cooperative offers an ideal structure through which modern agricultural practices, the result of modern research, can be applied most efficiently to local conditions. The results of such experiments may be fascinating and yet more important still is that the cooperators understand the experiment and acquire the new scientific knowledge which such an understanding implies.

Finally, there is no doubt that India is divided into two: rich and poor India. The division is so great that one side can hardly understand the other. The Centre believes that India is *one* nation and that, consequently no citizen can ignore the plight of large sections of *his* nation. From this point of view, there is no difference between the so-called "insider" and "outsider"; they are all Indians trying to improve the nation. True to this belief, the Centre has many young persons from rich India reaching out to the poor and making an effort to understand them. This education of the rich is as important to national development as the education of the poor. Awareness of, and concern for the problems of all, specially, those who are in greatest need is, the Centre believes, true patriotism.

APPENDIX I

CASTE IDEOLOGY*

The meaning of Ideology

Ideology, one would think, has to do with ideas and concepts and, therefore, cannot include components other than conceptual. However, modern writers look at ideology differently. Thus, Therborn (1980: 16) defines ideology as discourse embedded in practice "which forms man's subjectivity". Subjectivity, he says is not coterminous with 'character' or 'personality' or 'social role'. "A person," says Therborn, "acts out, lives his/her personality as a subject, in different forms of subjectivity, which nevertheless do not exhaust it. Under certain conditions, the two may even come into tension or conflict. The forms of human subjectivity are constituted by intersections of the psychic and the social, and may be seen as the outer, more conscious, and more socially changeable aspects of the person."

Ideologies form a person's subjectivity because they give meaning and help the individual make sense of ordinary day-to-day existence, because they explain to him the way he lives his life in terms of ultimate principles (what exists), what is good or desirable and what is possible.

Therborn distinguishes them in terms of four areas of meaning:

1. *Existential-inclusive* ideologies relate to the eternal verities and create a sense of identity which touches the core of a person's being. They explain the meaning of the universe, of life and death. The great religions or even secular ideologies like historical materialism are examples. They claim exclusiveness in their possession of the truth and universality in their applicability.

---

* The ideas of this appendix were first published in a paper entitled: "Indian Socio-Cultural Reality: A Social Psychology Perspective" in PATIL, Kuncheria, (1987) *Socio-cultural Analysis in Theologizing*, Indian Theological Association, Bangalore, pp. 45 & ff.

2. *Historical-inclusive* ideologies form individuals to become members of historical social worlds. Such, for instance, are nationalist or ethnic ideologies.

3. *Existential-positional* ideologies are based on biological differences such as sex and age; for instance, ideologies of male chauvinism or feminism, or ideologies which privilege the young adult over the child and the aged.

4. *Historical-positional* ideologies form individuals to accept particular positions in a social group. Such, for instance are class ideologies, or ideologies relating to job positions.

As Therborn is careful to stress, the above distinctions are analytical. "They do not represent ideologies as they concretely appear and are labelled in everyday language. These may exhibit more than "one of the four dimensions, either at the same time or in different contexts," as caste ideology does.

5. *Ego- and alter-ideologies.* Positional ideologies have an intrinsically dual character: they explain what one is (ego-ideology) and how one relates to the Other (alter-ideology). Thus male chauvinism is an Ego-ideology as far as men are concerned, but alter-ideology defining women.

Inclusive ideologies have an alter component in their exclusion of others.

Caste as an Ideology

1. *Caste as an existential-inclusive ideology.* Many students of the caste system have associated it "with an autonomous form of cultural system or world-view" (Singh,1980: 6). M.N. Srinivas (1962: 150-151) writes:

It is impossible to detach Hinduism from the caste system. According to orthodox Hindu belief, mentioned for the first time in Rigvedic hymn *Purushasukta*, the four *varnas* or orders formed the limbs of primeval man (Purusha), who was victim in the divine sacrifice which produced the cosmos ...

Further, certain theological ideas such as rebirth *(samsara)*, the idea that the deeds done by an individual determine his position in the next birth *(karma)*, *papa* (sin), *punya* (merit), *moksha* (salvation) and *dharma* (morality) are intimately related to the caste system. . .the idea of *karma* teaches a Hindu that he is born into a particular caste because of certain actions performed in a previous life. The Dharmasutra mentions that if a man does good deeds he will be born in a high caste and be well endowed, while if he does sinful acts, he will be born in a low caste, or even as an animal – a pig or a donkey . . .

Birth in a particular caste becomes, therefore, an index of a soul's progress towards God. *Dharma*, the total body of moral and religious rules, is to some extent identified with the duties of one's caste – and this not only by the common people but in works of great influence like the *Bhagvadgita*.

Elsewhere he writes that hierarchy is based on the concept of pollution or ritual status. "This concept is absolutely fundamental to the caste system, and along with concepts of *karma* and *dharma* it contributes to make caste the unique institution it is."

Thus understood, the caste system is an existential-inclusive ideology which gives meaning to being in the world, to life and suffering. It defines what is good and what is possible in human existence. The advent of democracy and the initial stress on secularism and, above all the scientific temper have to a large extent, eroded the main elements of caste as an inclusive ideology. However, this does not mean that it has disappeared altogether: one has to reckon with it still, specially in rural India.

2. *The caste system as a historical-inclusive ideology*. Caste ideology is historical-inclusive on two counts: first, like any other religious ideology it sets its members apart from those of other religions. Second, it makes individuals conscious members of a particular *varna* and, consequently, of a particular state of purity and of a specific stage on their way to salvation.

Since ideology is *inclusive* it is also an ideology of *exclusion*: it separates the *twice-born* from the Shudras and (what remains an intractable problem) the caste people from those outside the pale of caste – the scheduled castes.

3. *Caste as historical-positional ideology*. Caste ideology may be rejected as an inclusive ideology and still it may be accepted as a historical-positional one. Many people delude themselves into thinking that they have rejected casteism simply because they no longer accept its 'inclusive' or 'sacral' elements. These people, like Srinivas,

see the caste system as so much part of Hinduism - an inclusive ideology – as to believe that secularisation will put an end to the caste system. But there are good reasons to believe that this may not happen (Kolenda, 1984). In any case, in the past, change of religion (hopefully rejection of the 'inclusive' elements of caste ideology) has not led to the abolition of casteism, it is evident from the history of Christianity in India.

Now caste as a historical-positional ideology makes an individual aware that he/she belongs to a specific group very clearly situated within the hierarchical pyramid of the caste system or, putting it more explicitly, an individual is proud to belong to an upper caste, and to that extent, looks down on the lower castes. One may refer to it as status. But what is status but the expression of a historical-positional ideology? Status is an evaluation made of oneself and others which must necessarily rely on norms which, in their turn, are part of society's understanding of itself. Status cannot be taken lightly: because if power enables the few to exploit others economically and politically, status can lead to a greater exploitation, the deprivation of social meaning, leading ultimately to the loss of self-respect. Therefore, there is power in status, Most people, unfortunately, respect themselves to the extent· to which they are respected by others and, worse still, when they are despised by others they end up by despising themselves.

Subjectivity Formation

Having examined the meaning of ideology, let us now turn to study how ideologies shape man's subjectivity. Very vivid personal experiences may give rise to an understanding of life and consequently to a set of values which are very different from the rest of society. Such individuals often set up counter-cultures or a philosophy and values which run counter to the commonly accepted ones. Still the majority of ordinary mortals are mass-assembled. It is worth studying how this assembly line works, or how the subjectivity of individuals is formed. In this process three elements can be observed: the external factors which set this process in motion, the process itself and the result.

1. *The external factors* which shape the subjectivity of individuals may be a set of formal doctrines (more commonly referred to as ideology); they may also be those general beliefs, behavioural norms,

values and ideals, which exist in a folk culture which are transmitted orally and more powerfully through symbols and the very behavioural patterns of the groups in question. Important external factors are the individuals themselves, the groups to which they belong, the organisations they have set up or inherited. External factors are the houses where people live and the location of those houses, the forms of salutation, rules of comensality, language itself and the gestures and facial expressions inasmuch as they show appreciation or contempt of others. Individuals, groups, and organisations interact among themselves and transmit effectively although unconsciously the meaning and values of the powerful groups.

2. *The process* begins at birth. Infancy plays a very critical role in forming the subjectivity of individuals all the more so since it shapes the unconscious wherefrom values often spring. It is difficult to understand some of the caste and communal prejudices unless one takes into consideration the contempt and revulsion assimilated by the infant unconscious.

Fortunately, the process does not stop there, it goes on for the rest of a person's life. In this process two subjective responses are possible. One is that of a person who is so conditioned by society as to accept without questioning the meaning and values given to him; the other possibility presupposes a critical attitude which questions what society proclaims. In the former case man's subjectivity is formed by others while in the latter a person forms it himself. Society conditions man, no doubt; but man can shape himself and his own destiny to some extent. Unless this latter possibility is accepted theoretically, at least, man is reduced to the proverbial cog in a machine, and the possibility of change is left entirely to forces beyond his control.

The process of subjectivity formation leads to both subjection and qualification which turn the individual into a functional member of the existing society.

Subjection takes place when an individual accepts the meaning and values of society. In so doing he accepts unconsciously, and therefore very effectively, *that society* and his position in it. Since this process of subjection is so important, it deserves closer scrutiny. Groups use ideology to discipline, i.e. to bring under control and to train individual members. This they achieve in two ways: one is *discursive*, i.e., an appeal to the intellect obviously at the conscious level; the other is *non-discursive*, or an appeal to feelings and also to the imagination addressed mainly to the unconscious. Let us take up the last first.

The Formation of the Unconscious

The unconscious, psychologists tell us, is made accessible to us mainly through feelings and the imagination. Caste ideology appeals to both in the following manner:

1. *The use of language.* Ordinary language makes generous use of adjectives like backward, impure, etc. which carry affective connotations and are likely to elicit and reinforce feelings of dislike or contempt. The vernacular has many words specifically meant to denote the inferior castes. The sentiments thus produced make some feel superior and others inferior. Opposite feelings can be aroused by words like pure, educated, rich, etc.

Apart from words, the manner of speaking itself may have a similar effect. But this is intimately related to the next point.

2. *Gestures and symbols* also have a forceful impact on our feelings and imagination. A gesture of superiority or contempt like making the other stand at a distance, sit in a lower place, the act of throwing things at someone rather than placing them in his hand — all these manifest dislike or contempt of the other. Ridicule, of course, is another such expression. The way dwellings in a village are arranged, is also highly symbolical and conveys the same idea.

On the other hand, touching another's feet, offering him a higher place to sit and so on are ways of showing deference and are likely to evoke feelings of respect, appreciation or admiration.

Language, gestures, symbols result directly from caste ideology and reinforce it much more effectively in that they are not discursive and, consequently, are not censured by the intellect — they directly impact our unconscious.

The Subjection of the Intellect

However, when man wants something, he finds it easy to convince even his intellect. Ideology is a convenient tool used by society to convince the intellect that everything is all right. At its most devastating, ideology can so blind reason as to prevent it from seeing anything but the world it presents. Caste ideology convinces a

Harijan that his world is a natural one and that, therefore, there is no other form of existence for him. Ideology tells the upper castes that there is a hierarchy of castes, some high, others low. By telling them what exists it also tells them what does not exist — exploitation, the degradation of the lowest castes, etc. etc.

When education and social awareness make people realise that the caste system is man-made and that what man creates man can also destroy, a second line of defence is used: "for all its shortcomings, the caste system is good." "There is exploitation because the lower castes are not sufficiently educated. And, certain people have to be treated sternly or else they will remain lazy, dirty, spending their money on drink."

A more critical understanding of society may lead to the realisation that there is something intrinsically evil in branding people low simply because of birth. At this stage, the defenders of the system fall back on their third line of defence: "True, casteism must be abolished; but this cannot be done with a stroke of the pen. Given the immensity of our country, more than one hundred thousand villages and a population exceeding 700 million, given the various stages of educational, economic and social development at which people are (one can easily wax eloquent), caste prejudices cannot be rooted out overnight. Let us be practical and accept the present situation as it is. Let us give it time. One is not bound to do impossible things." The problem with this line of reasoning is that it is often a cover for inactivity.

Qualification

Groups, like individuals, have a survival instinct and take steps to perpetuate themselves. Disciplining members into accepting the norms of the group is one way to do it. But it is not enough. Efficiency demands that all members be trained to play their roles; the stability of the system, in traditional societies, requires that nobody should be qualified to carry out tasks higher than the ones assigned to him. The wisdom of this policy was well understood in olden times. We are told by the Mandal commission (Mehta, Patel, 1985: 306), that Ekalavya, a tribal boy, lost his right thumb on the orders of his Guru Dronacharya, because the poor boy wanted to learn the art of archery (*dhanurvidya*); and that Shambuk, a Shudra, was beheaded by Rama for attempting meditation. When subjection is not matched by corresponding qualification the stability and, consequently, the permanence of the system are threatened.

In this context, one can see that the most serious and organised attempt our government has made to fight casteism has been to set up the system of reservations. It not only enables and facilitates the learning of new skills which will qualify the scheduled castes for posts and professions formerly reserved to the upper castes; but it actually opens the doors of such profession to them. As the Mandal commission puts it:

> . . . we must recognise that an essential part of the battle against social backwardness is to be fought in the minds of the backward people. In India, government service has always been looked upon as a symbol of prestige and power. By increasing the representation of OBCs (other backward castes) in government services, we give them an immediate feeling of participation in the governance of this country. When a backward class candidate becomes a collector or a superintendent of police, the material benefits accruing from his position are limited to the members of his family only. But the psychological spin-off of this phenomenon is tremendous: the entire community of that backward class candidate feels socially elevated, (Mehta, Patel, 1985: 306).

Of course, there are material benefits accruing to a backward class even as a group, from such appointments; even a police sub-inspector can be very effective in preventing the injustices heaped upon his own brethren by the upper caste Hindus (a task which his upper caste colleague is more likely to ignore). In the long run, the whole ethos of the government bureaucracy is bound to turn more favourable to scheduled castes and other weaker sections of society once its composition changes from a virtual monopoly of the high castes into a more balanced representation of the whole population.

3. *The result* of the processes of subjection and qualification described earlier is, as far as society is concerned, the maintenance of the *status quo*. In a society where injustices abound, acceptance of its values (its ideology) is tantamount to accepting its injustices; because ideology in such a case serves to legitimize what is morally wrong.

The result, as far as individuals are concerned, is subjection. Ideologies enslave people to a greater or less degree. And yet, there can be no organisation without an ideology. As Debray (1983: 140) put it, "Whenever a *we* gets under way, there is an ideology." True liberation in this sense can be achieved either by an immediate experience of God which goes beyond concepts or by a perfect state of awareness. "If ideologies are ways of organising ourselves in the world and not ways of seeing the world, the key to the logic of ideology is to be found in the logic of organisation." (Laclau, 1977: 169)

It has been mentioned earlier that a passive formation of one's subjectivity leads to subjection. Now the extent of subjection varies depending on economic, social and educational factors. Abject poverty, economic overdependence and lack of educational opportunities with the resultant low status in society lead to the worst type of subjection. Freire (1972) calls it a state of semi-intransitive or magical consciousness. W.A. Smith (1976) summarises his thought:

Magical consciousness is characterised by acceptance and resignation in the face of brutality and over oppression. It is typified by silence; by very short responses to very complex questions; by simplistic causal relationships; and by the absence of guilt (p. 37).

Individuals at this stage of consciousness are trapped by the "myth of natural inferiority." "They know that they do things, what they do not know is that man's actions as such are transforming" (Freire, 1972: 30). It is this sense of impotence which prevents individuals from naming their problems in dehumanizing terms, which ties them to magical explanations, and which limits their activities to passive acceptance. Rather than resisting or changing the reality in which they find themselves, they conform to it (p. 45).

As a result people in this stage of consciousness tend to *deny* that they have any problems. If they do admit to having problems they define them in terms of biological survival.

Men of semi-intransitive consciousness cannot apprehend problems situated outside their sphere of biological necessity. Their interests centre almost totally around survival, and they lack a sense of life on a more historic plane. . . In this sense only, semi-intransitivity represents a near disengagement between men and their existence (Freire, 1973: 17).

It is because men are so far removed from existence that they fail to see unemployment, poor health, malnutrition as problems. They are simply 'facts of life' which one must learn to accept because nothing can be done about them. Such an individual "simply apprehends facts and attributes to them a superior power by which it is controlled and to which it must therefore submit" (Freire, 1973: 44).

Smith (1976: 48) clarifies this point further:

The individuals who are unable to perceive their condition as problematic, but rather as simply a composite of facts over which they have no control, generally rely on some external forces to define and alter those facts. *God*, *fate*, *luck*, the *times* all play this role. It is important here to distinguish between a fatalistic dependence on a superior power which leads to a numbing passivity and is considered magical, and a genuine belief in the existence of a superior power which can release powerful spiritual resources within an individual and is considered critical . . . .

Neither a belief in God, nor humility in the face of God characterizes mythical consciousness, but rather a dependence on God for action, and a denial of the human capacity to act with God to change events. A classic cliche is appropriate here, "God helps those who help themselves."

Naive consciousness is a higher stage than magical consciousness and yet one in which man's potentiality remains severely curtailed. True, passivity gives way to action but one which attacks the symptoms rather than the causes of the disease. There is a romantic, and nostalgic looking back at the past "when things were better," there is a "strong tendency to gregariousness: and the practice of polemics rather than dialogue" (Freire, 1973: 18). To quote Smith again,

> Oppressed individuals at the naive level of consciousness accept that something is wrong. They can identify specific injustices and relate long stories of how they are exploited. But their understanding does not go beyond blaming individuals. They fail to see that a system of powerful forces act together to coerce both the oppressed and the oppressor. They naively, romantically, nostalgically assume that individuals are basically free agents, independent of the socio-economic system in which they live.

Chafing under the strain of an unjust order and lacking the vision of, and the faith in the need to attack the root causes, they are likely to feel frustrated and angry and often turn their anger against their own brethren, their co-sufferers; or, more pathetically still, against themselves and their family — self-hatred leading to self-punishment.

Having accepted the values and meaning of society, the oppressed admire and would like to be like the upper castes. And so, on the one hand, they are themselves and, on the other, they are their oppressors whose image they have internalised. This dual existence prevents them from having self-respect and respect and appreciation of their caste brethren - the upper castes alone are worthy individuals. Under such circumstances, it is very easy for an upper caste leader to keep the scheduled castes divided. Without self-respect unity remains elusive.

Again, being despised by the upper castes, the lower ones learn to despise those still lower in the hierarchy. If unity within the same caste is difficult, unity and cooperation among various castes appears to be unattainable.

The above refers to the lower castes. How does an uncritical acceptance of the meaning and values of society affect the upper castes? First, of course, it suits them well, it pacifies their conscience and drives away any guilt they might otherwise feel. "They have a right to their position in society." This may be very convenient as far as the enjoyment of material comforts is concerned; but, as far as their mental development goes, they too are enslaved in a magical or naive consciousness. Somebody has spoken of our 'illiterate scientists' and the same adjective can describe the other professions as well.

The Evils of Caste Ideology

1. *Caste ideology divides the poor.* The only power and the only strength poor people have lies in their numbers. But this presupposes unity and cooperation which caste ideology very effectively prevents. In most of our smaller villages, except for a few relatively well-to-do families, all the others irrespective of their caste are poor. Their economic interests, therefore, are the same. The need of unity and the advantages of cooperation are there for all to see. But their subjectivity has been so formed (or de-formed) that an upper caste person may find it psychologically impossible to join hands with a Harijan. Clever upper-caste leaders make sure that even the Harijans themselves remain divided. The caste system makes it very easy for such leaders to manipulate the lower castes.

2. *Caste ideology distorts the perception of reality.* The exploited, ranked low in the caste hierarchy, being constantly despised, treated with contempt either in a crude or subtle manner, end up by interiorising that image and believing that they are lower. Having accepted the others as higher, they behave accordingly: giving them respect, deference, and honour, accepting their claims and, in the process, reinforcing the whole exploitative cycle. The reality, of course, is that they are *not* lower. Caste ideology has deformed their subjectivity which then distorts their perception of reality to their great personal and social disadvantage.

The upper caste poor are taught by caste ideology to take pride in their caste and to set themselves apart from the rest of the poor, thereby remaining inevitably bound to the upper caste rich. Were they to join hands with all the poor, not only would they emancipate themselves from that subjection, but they would easily become the leaders of a new movement, thereby improving both their economic and their socio-political status. Unfortunately, caste ideology prevents them from seeing and understanding reality.

3. *Caste ideology upholds injustice.* Through the various mechanisms described earlier caste ideology silences the conscience of the citizens by reassuring them that the existing misery is not their own fault and that their heartlessness is morally right. But for this justification, they would lack the moral strength to watch human

suffering with a detachment with which they watch natural events. It is not true that caste evils are upheld by power alone. Since men are rational and moral beings, force alone cannot be the basis of their relationships. In the final analysis, it is ideology that sustains the unjust social structure by ensuring the very sufferers' consent to their own suffering.

4. *Caste ideology is itself exploitative.* Even at the risk of being repetitive, it is necessary to stress this point. Caste ideology creates millions of alienated, unworthy persons, who are unwilling to identify, with themselves and try to be like somebody else. Psychologists call this an inferiority complex, activists call it an interiorisation of the exploiter's image, Marx refers to it as alienation. These are labels, more or less apt, to explain the situation. But the reality is that all this produces untold suffering, where it hurts most: in the inner self. This suffering and wrong understanding of self then block personal growth and do not allow existing potentialities to come to fruition. Any attempt to change social relations or their underlying socio-economic structure which ignores ideology, fails to take an essential factor into consideration and, to that extent, is bound to be less effective.

A TRIBAL ANIMAL HEALTH CARE SYSTEM*

Gujarat has a large tribal population concentrated along the hilly areas on its eastern border. The tribals constitute about 14 per cent of the population in the state; but they are more than 90 per cent in the Dangs district and are an important part of the population in three other districts (see Table 13), where they are in the majority in the eastern talukas.

Table 13: **Districts in Gujarat with Sizeable Tribal Population**

Rank	District	Per cent
1.	Dangs	92.55
2.	Surat	49.97
3.	Broach	41.59
4.	Panchmahals	34.26
5.	Baroda	21.47
6.	Sabarkantha	13.94

Source: 1961 Census.

These tribals have led their own autonomous and, in ages past, fairly self-sufficient lives. But as the trees were felled and the forests where they lived began to disappear, their livelihood vanished together with them and their subsistence was threatened. Both the central and the state governments have floated many schemes to help the tribals, similar to those for the scheduled castes.

One of the welfare programmes of the Government of Gujarat is a scheme which grants the tribals a 50 per cent subsidy to buy buffaloes or cows. Commercial banks match this grant with soft loans to cover the rest of the cost. Under this scheme, many societies have brought large quantities of buffaloes into the tribal belt. This massive transfer has not been effected out of a genuine concern for the

---

* An edited version of the 1984 Annual Report on the TVW system.

tribals. Traders have benefited by buying old buffaloes and selling them at high prices. Officials have profited from the scheme by exacting their 'cut' from both traders and beneficiaries, bank officials have enriched themselves by demanding money to expedite loan. Rich farmers have found a way of disposing of old animals at remunerative prices. Even the district milk cooperatives had a stake in this scheme as it increased the milk production of their district – and their profits. Small wonder that such a scheme has become popular.

Apart from the problem of making good purchases and avoiding financial leakages, these societies faced another difficulty. The buffalo is a delicate animal which requires special care. There has been no tradition of buffalo rearing in this area and, therefore, the local population lacks the skills required for this task. Again, in remote areas veterinary services are not available. The massive transfer of milch cattle has strained the fodder resources.

The Centre's Involvement

The Centre, requested by several societies (Table 14) to help their Milk Producers' Cooperatives, identified two areas in which it could intervene: one was training in animal health care, the other was administrative help required to keep the accounts, the bureaucratic work required to secure grants, subsidies and good purchases of animals, and a control over the Union Dairy to see that the primary producers receive their due. Otherwise, the cooperatives deal directly with the Union Dairy at district headquarters where the milk is sold.

Some societies run just one cooperative which groups several villages together (in the case of Dediapada 40), collect the milk, transport it and sell it to the Union Dairy. The office of these cooperatives takes upon itself the following duties:

1. The collection of milk from individual members through collection centres.
2. Testing samples to determine the percentage of fat in the milk delivered.
3. Transportation of milk from the villages and sale to the Union Dairy.

4. Payment to each individual according to the quality and quantity of milk he delivers.
5. Purchase of cattle feed, vaccines, medicines and their distribution and sale to individual cooperative members.
6. Maintenance of records and accounts.
7. Dealing with banks, insurance companies, government officials.

Table 14: **List of Societies Involved in the Project**

Society	Village	Taluka	District
Adivasi Pragati Kendra	Vyara	Vyara	Surat
Samaj Seva Sangh	Zhankhvav	Mangrol	Surat
Adivasi Samaj Seva Kendra	Sagbara	Sagbara	Broach
Bharuch Social Service Society	Jagadia	Jagadia	Broach
Dediapada Social Service Society	Dediapada	Dediapada	Broach
Catholic Church	Dharampur	Dharampur	Bulsar
Jivan Jyot Social Service Society	Pimpri		Dangs

The efficient running of these cooperatives depends on their personnel and, more specifically, on their administration, management and values. Management includes a critical evaluation of the cooperative's performance in production, first; its relations with the individual members, second; and, finally, the relations of the cooperative with the Union Dairy. This evaluation, keeping in mind present legislation and market forces, should lead to better planning in the future. Values here mean honesty and the will to act in the interests of the majority of the producers.

In other words, the cooperative has three roles to play:

1. *A protective role* i.e. to protect the interests of the primary producer by preserving and increasing his animal wealth and by securing the best price for his milk.

2. *An active role* of building up the assets of the whole cooperative. In a centralised cooperative there is always the danger of using revenues to acquire non-productive assets to the detriment of productive ones like fodder, an animal health care system and other measures aimed at the genetic improvement of the herd.

3. *An educative role* which includes the setting up of a good buffalo rearing tradition and developing a true understanding of the goals and working of the cooperative.

One of the aims of these milk cooperatives is to raise the economic standard of their members. This means that the milch cattle must yield enough milk to earn a revenue sufficient not only to cover the costs and investment but also to give the owner a reasonable income.

Two factors are critical: price and milk yield. The former is determined by the Union Cooperative. All that the local cooperative can do is to reduce its overhead expenditure so as to minimize the cuts on the money paid to the primary producer.

The following things can be done to increase the milk yield:

1. Make sure that good buffaloes are purchased.
2. Set up an efficient animal health care system.
3. Educate the primary producer and thus help him/her to establish a good animal husbandry tradition.
4. Improve the nutrition of the animals.
5. A long-range measure is, of course, genetic improvement.

The Centre's involvement with these cooperatives was limited to seting up an animal health care system and through it to help build up a good buffalo-rearing tradition.

An Animal Health Care System

TVW stands for Tribal Village Worker. Since the National Dairy Development Board through the Indian Dairy Corporation partially subsidised this scheme, the right acronym to define the beneficiaries of the grant had to be used. TVW stands now in about a hundred villages for a para-veterinarian or, in the local language, for the "buffalo doctor."

The need for such a system arose from the fact that villages in the interior lacked any medical facilities. It was almost impossible to secure the services of trained veterinary doctors. Another factor has been mentioned earlier: new owners of buffaloes did not know how to take care of them. The initial plan had been to teach animal husbandry in each village. But the cost in time and money involved and the meagre results dissuaded the Centre from such an approach. It was decided to concentrate all effort on the training and continued guidance of the TVWs.

Training of Para-Veterinary Personnel

A summary of the training activities involved in this programme is given in Table 15. In the foundation course, the TVW is given fundamental theoretical inputs and actual practice on animals. This course lasts three months. It is a residential course and is conducted by the Xavier Agricultural Training Centre at Mogar, a village close to Anand where the so-called "White Revolution" started. Each course takes 15 students only. Personal attention and, specially, a lot of supervised practice make it necessary to keep the numbers down.

Table 15: **Training Programme of the TVWs**

No.	Training Activity	Time	Duration	Place
1.	Foundation course	At the start	3 months	Mogar
2.	Personal follow-up	Weekly	One day	TVW's village
3.	Meetings	Monthly	One day	Coop. office
4.	Short refresher courses	2-3 a year	3 days	Fokadi/Vyara/Pimpri
5.	Long refresher course	After 1-2 yrs.	10 days/3 months	Mogar
6.	General education	Once	10 days	St. Xavier's Ahmedabad

Village people who have only finished primary school cannot remain profitably at their studies for more than three months. On the other hand, this is too short a period to master all the intricacies of veterinary work. As they return to their villages they are easily assailed by doubts − is this the proper medicine to be used in this case? Diffident about their own skills, they are afraid. Something may go wrong, they may not be accepted by their own people. The Centre's doctor begins the second phase of the training, dispelling doubts and allaying the fears of the TVWs.

The doctor's presence is also required to withstand the resistance of other villagers. A traditional and hierarchical society does not easily accept that a younger, possibly poorer, and hardly educated member of its own village can be a competent animal doctor. Elderly people are not likely to entrust precious cattle to a younger person simply because he has been three months out of the village. To make matters worse, modern practices like vaccination, artificial insemination and pregnancy detection tests may be looked upon with great suspicion if not downright hostility. To overcome these prejudices is the task of an experienced and qualified doctor who has the patience to listen to all the questions of the villagers and the ability to answer them to their satisfaction. He can open the door to new practices and he can legitimise the role of the TVW.

TVW and doctor work together for some time. The former doing most of the work, the latter standing by and coming to his rescue if necessary. With the doctor by his side, the TVW loses his fear; by doing things himself, he gains confidence. In the process, the other farmers grow accustomed to seeing him work. As the TVW's confidence increases, so does his joy and his eagerness to work. His availability and readiness to work win the goodwill of the formerly suspicious farmers. The system is now fully operational.

Even fully trained doctors need to upgrade their knowledge; these para-vets all the more so. What is not daily practised is easily forgotten; there are diseases which are seasonal; the first cases may catch the TVW unawares. As the doctor moves from village to village, he realises what lessons have to be repeated. This is done during the monthly meetings or, if need be, a refresher course.

Competence is necessary but not sufficient. The greater the experience, or the better the skills, the greater the power and prestige of the TVW. In some villages he is also the cooperative official who receives and measures the milk brought by the individual members and prepares the village cans to be taken to the Union Dairy. It is easy for him to add water to the milk and earn a few extra rupees. A very competent but dishonest official can easily make a good additional income at the expense of the others. As para-vet he can also demand money for his services and, what is worse, prescribe unnecessary medicines and collect additional charges. A good animal health care system demands the right values and attitudes.

A team spirit and a well-developed sense of identity with the new health care system can help withstand the undeniable social pressures leading to corruption. The monthly meetings and occasional courses in which all the TVWs of the same area participate are meant to strengthen and further develop this *esprit de corps*. The idea is to prevent a TVW from feeling isolated in his village, by communicating the fellowship and support of the whole group.

A competent and honest TVW can easily help his people not only in the veterinary but also in other fields. Indeed, many TVWs are now helping other villagers with the insurance companies, the banks,

the bureaucracy. Awareness in one area leads to an all-round awareness. The ability to handle the animal health care system qualifies
them to deal with other organisational matters.

The last training activity listed in Table 15 is a ten-day course on
general education with special emphasis on three different areas: (1)
general knowledge, (2) proper attitudes and (3) concrete skills.

1. *General knowledge*. A quick survey of the evolution of man and
of the various systems in which he moves, the family, society, political, economic, industrial and educational organisations. The aim of
this section is double, first to increase the TVWs general knowledge
and, second, to convey the idea that man has always been on the
move, that there is progress everywhere. The second part of this section is meant to raise their social awareness; it deals with the socio-
economic structures in India with special reference to those which
affect the tribals more closely. This serves as an introduction to the
next section.

2. *Right attitudes* like self-respect, pride in tribal culture, pride in
their own brethren, unity and cooperation, are inculcated.

3. *Skills* are also imparted concurrently, the most important one
being arithmetic which they need to keep the accounts of the
cooperative, to calculate the price of the milk according to percentage of fat, etc. There are also exercises in public speaking and others
meant to improve their communication skills.

The result of the educational efforts has been the formation of an
able cadre of para-veterinarians, as the explanation of the services
rendered by them will clearly show.

Veterinary Services of the TVWs

There are five different types of services provided by the TVWs:
(1) Prevention of disease, (2) curative services, (3) care of newborn
calves, (4) services related to breeding and (5) maintenance of
records.

Prevention of disease : Vaccinations. Timely vaccination is of critical importance to avoid epidemics which may cause either the death
or grave impairment of productive capacity. Vaccinations were ad-
ministered earlier by either the veterinary doctor or the livestock in-
spector of the animal husbandry department. They are now taken
care of by the TVWs on a very wide and systematic basis, according
to the schedule in Table 16.

Table 16 : **Vaccination Schedule of the TVWs**

Disease	Time	Source of Supply	Remarks
Foot & Mouth	March & Sept.	Union Dairy	Bought by individual members*
Hemorrhagic Septicemia	May-June	State Government	Free of charge
Black Quarters	May-June	State Government	Free of charge

N.B. Anthrax vaccination is also given in some places.
* The Dediapada Cooperative gives it free of charge.

The TVW's vaccination work has two advantages: first, the cooperative need not worry about calling doctors or other trained staff to vaccinate the animals. Secondly, the TVWs make sure that all the animals in all the villages are vaccinated and they maintain vaccination records. The cooperative officials can easily check the work done.

Curative services. Some Union Dairies make provision for round-the-clock veterinary services. But in remote tribal villages these services are either not available or are very expensive. The new animal health care system run by the TVWs treats 60 per cent of the medical cases. Of the 100 TVWs who have been practising, 10 have shown special ability and have been given advanced training. These senior TVWs can take care of an additional 20 per cent, leaving to the doctor only the most difficult cases.

Tables 17 and 18 list the medical cases treated by the TVWs and the medicines used. The medicines are bought by the cooperative, and handed over to the TVWs who administer them and recover the costs from the owner of the buffalo treated. Prompt attention is critical in many cases. The presence of the TVW in the village with a ready stock of medicines provides quick service in times of emergency. Such cases are underlined in Table 17.

Special care of newborn calves. Calf mortality can cause disturbances in the lactation of buffaloes, specially when they are in the hands of inexperienced people. Female calf mortality, moreover, affects the stability and self-sufficiency of the cooperative. The care of calves is therefore important. This care starts during the last two months of pregnancy. At this time the mother must be fed with concentrates. The care taken after birth is shown in Table 19.

Table 17: **Medical Cases Treated by the TVWs**

No.	Medical Case	% of Affected Animals	Remarks
1.	Simple Indigestion	24	
2.	*Tympany (Bloat)*	12	Common during early rains
3.	Impaction of Rumen	10	Severe cases require a doctor
4.	Oral injuries	8	Common during the dry season
5.	Enteritis	8	
6.	Bovine Surra	6	Medicine kept with Sr TVW
7.	Hoof injuries	42	Very common during the monsoon
8.	*Mastitis (Teat injuries)*	8	Prompt treatment maintains milk yield
9.	Milk let down problems	5	—do—
10.	*Dystocia (Mal-presentation of fetus)*	1.8	Prompt correction saves mother and calf.
11.	Retention of placenta	3	Prompt treatment avoids future reproductive problems
12.	Prolapse of uterus	2	
13.	Mineral deficiencies and anemia	15	Nutritional deficiencies and parasitic anemia
14.	Accidents, horn in-juries/minor abrasions		Sporadic occurrence
15.	Systemic disturbances: Toxemia, milk fever etc.		Sporadic occurrence

Services related to breeding activities. Regular calving is necessary if the milk yield is to be maintained and, if possible increased. The breeding season is critical in dairy farming. The activities of the TVWs during that time include (1) special care of the buffalo bulls (feeding them with concentrates and keeping them tied to regulate their services), (2) detection of heat, (3) artificial insemination where the facilities are available, (4) detection of pregnancy and (5) treatment of buffaloes not coming in heat.

Table 18: **List of Medicines with the TVWs**

1.	Tincture iodine	2.	Tincture Benzoin
3.	Turpentine oil	4.	BHC powder
5.	Dressing powder	6.	Antiseptic solution
7.	Magnesium sulphate	8.	Sodium bicarbonate
9.	Astringent powders	10.	Tonic mixtures
11.	Oxytocin ampoules	12.	Mineral mixtures
13.	Deworming agents (for calves)		
14.	Antibiotic boluses (Treatment of calf diarrhoea and uterine problems)		

Table 19: **Calf Care Schedule**

Age in days	Feeding	Treatment
1	Colostrum 5 to 7 times	Tincture iodine on navel
2	— do —	Antibiotic bolus
3	Colostrum	Deworming dose
7	Milk	— do —
30	— do —	— do —

Those who receive a buffalo for the first time must be taught to detect the signs of heat in her in order to avoid long dry periods when, naturally, the buffalo is not productive. During the last months of the breeding season, the TVWs are always on the move making sure that all buffaloes are inseminated, specially those which are long overdue. Failure to do it during these months means delaying the lactation for another year. The cowherds are the main target of the TVW's questioning, although the owners are not excluded. This persistent questioning and explaining has raised the awareness of the primary producer, thereby reducing both the dry periods and the tasks of the TVW.

Artificial insemination, wherever facilities to preserve the frozen semen exist, is promoted to improve the herd genetically.

Not all the buffaloes which have been inseminated become pregnant. Such failures should be detected early when the buffaloes can be inseminated a second time.

Maintenance of records. These tasks can be best carried out if records are kept regularly and accurately. These records facilitate the work of both the doctor and the cooperative officials. Table 20 shows the types of entries in the main record book kept by each TVW in his village.

Table 20: **List of Buffaloes and Relevant Information on them**

No.	Owner	Buffalo's name	No. of calvings	Last calvings	Insemination	PD	Calving Exp	Act	Calf M/F	Vacc.	Remark
1	2	3	4	5	6	7	8	9	10	11	12

The number of calvings in column 4 indicates also the age of the buffalo. Buffaloes have their first calving in this area when they are about four years old. Subsequent calvings may take place after 14 months; in practice however, every second year. Columns 5 through 7 tell the TVW what kind of attention each buffalo requires.

A summary of these records is submitted every month to the doctor in charge of the whole Animal Health Care System and to the cooperative officials for their study.

The TVWs Educate the Primary Producers

The efforts of this project have now provided one person in 60 villages who has a sound and scientific knowledge of animal husbandry. However, this is not enough. The aim is to have all the cooperators possess the required knowledge, as well. This is the task of the TVW himself who, as he moves around treating diseased cattle, examining animals which need to be inseminated, or taking care of recently calved buffaloes, explains to the owners and their wives (who do most of the work) the essentials of animal husbandry in the language which they best understand. When the payment of the milk comes, he has another opportunity to explain how the price of milk is fixed: the importance of the fat percentage and how the quality of milk may be improved. Or it may just be through idle talk at the end of the day when several families sit out, smoking the hookah and whiling away the time: why some owners receive a high income and others no income at all, breeding difficulties, nutrition problems and possible solutions. Could lucerne be grown in part of the village's pasture land? Could silos be built to preserve the abundant grass of the monsoon? Could they all grow some fodder trees in their backyards? They are not conventional lectures but ordinary conversations. The results are not instantaneous and flashy; but they can be appreciated over a long period of time. This is a quiet but efficient transfer of technology.

The Centre's concern has been education. Scientific and technological knowledge is an important part of education. It is not the only one, granted; it may not even be the most important, may be; but it is important, all the same. Cynics often say that scientific education cannot be imparted to poor people. The TVW system set up in a backward and poor region, proves that education *can* be imparted. It also proves that it cannot be improvised and handed over within a couple of days. It takes time and professional dedication. Those who educate must first know the people, their needs, and` their temperaments in order to ascertain what new technology is required and how it is to be explained. The educator must also master his own discipline to know exactly what can, what must, and what should not be told. In other words, a good educator knows what must be taught and how it is to be taught.

BIBLIOGRAPHY

BAVISKAR, B S (1980). *The Politics of Development. Sugar Cooperatives in Rural Maharashtra.* Delhi: Oxford University Press.

BEHAVIOURAL SCIENCE CENTRE (1977-78, 1978-79, 1979-80, 1980-81, 1981-82, 1982-83, 1983-84). *St. Xavier's Non-formal Education Society Annual Report.* Mimeo. Ahmedabad: St. Xavier's College.

BEHAVIOURAL SCIENCE CENTRE (1985-87). *St. Xavier's Non-formal Education Society Annual Report.* Anand: Anand Press.

BHAI, N P (1986). *Harijan Women in Independent India.* Delhi: B.R. Publishing Corporation.

BHATT, Anil (1975). *Caste, Class and Politics: An Empirical Profile of Social Stratification in Modern India.* Delhi: Manohar Book Service.

BOWEN E R (1953). *The Cooperative Road to Abundance. The Alternative to Monopolism and Communism.* New York: Henry Schuman.

BRADFORD, L P, GIBB, J R, BENNE, K D (1964). *T-Group Theory and Laboratory Method.* New York: John Wiley.

COX, Harvey (1966). *The Secular City.* New York: Macmillan Co.

DEBRAY, Regis (1983). *Critique of Political Reason.* London: Verso, NLB.

DESAI, I P (1976). *Untouchability in Rural Gujarat.* Bombay: Popular Prakashan.

DUSHKIN, Lelah (1972). "Scheduled Caste Politics" in J M Mahar *The Untouchables in Contemporary India.* Tucson: The University of Arizona Press.

EGAN, Gerard (1970). *Encounter: Group Processes for Interpersonal Growth.* Belmont,Ca.: Brooks/Cole Publishing Company.

ENGELMANN, Konrad (1968). *Building Cooperative Movements in Developing Countries. The sociological and psychological aspects.* New York: Frederick A. Praeger.

FREIRE, Paulo (1972). *Pedagogy of the Oppressed*. Hamondsworth: Penguin Books.

—— (1972a). *Cultural Action for Freedom*. Hamondsworth: Penguin Books.

—— (1973). *Education for Critical Consciousness*. New York: The Seabury Press.

GALANTER, Marc (1984). *Competing Equalities*. Berkeley: University of California Press.

GEORGE, Alexandra (1986). *Social Ferment in India*. London and Atlantic Highlands, N.J.: The Athlone Press.

GOLEMBIEWSKI, R T, BLUMBERG, A (1970). *Sensitivity Training and the Laboratory Approach*. Itasca, Ill.: F.E Peacock Publishers.

GOULD, Harold (1987). *The Hindu Caste System. The Sacralization of a Social Order*. New Delhi: Chanakya Publications. [Castes and Outcastes and the Sociology of Stratification, 73-103].

GREENBERG, E S (1986). *Workplace Democracy. The Political Effects of Participation*. Ithaca: Cornell University Press.

HELM F C (1968). *The Economics of Cooperative Enterprise*. London: University of London Press.

HEREDERO, J M (1977). *Rural Development and Social Change. An Experiment in Non-Formal Education*. Columbia, South Asia Books.

ILLICH, I D (1971). *Deschooling Society*. New York: Harper & Row.

IMPERIAL GAZETTEERS OF INDIA (1908). Oxford: The Clarendon Press.

JOSHI, B R (1982). *Democracy in Search of Equality: Untouchable Politics and Indian Social Change*. Delhi: Hindustan Publishing Corporation.

JOSHI, Barbara (ed.) (1986). *Untouchable! Voices from the Dalit Liberation Movement*. London: Zed Books.

KAMBLE, N D (1982). *The Scheduled Castes*. New Delhi: Ashish Publishing House.

KHARE, R S (1984). *The Untouchable as Himself: Ideology, Identity and Pragmatism among the Lucknow Chamars*. Cambridge: Cambridge University Press.

KOLENDA, Pauline (1984). *Caste in Contemporary India*. Jaipur: Rawat Publications.

KOTHARI, R (ed.) (1970). *Caste in Indian Politics*. Delhi: Orient Longman.

KOTHARI, R, MARU, R (1970). "Federating for Political Interests: The Kshatriyas of Gujarat" in KOTHARI, R. (ed.), *Caste in Indian Politics*. Delhi: Orient Longman.

KSHIRSAGAR, R K (1986). *Untouchability in India. Implementation of the Law of its Abolition*. Delhi: Deep & Deep.

KURIAN V M (1986). *Caste-class Formation*. Delhi: B.R. Publishing Corporation. [Study of the Syrian Christians and the Backward Christians.]

MAHAR, Michael J (ed.) (1972). *The Untouchables in Contemporary India*. Tucson: The University of Arizona Press.

MEHTA, H, PATEL H. (Eds.) (1985). *Dynamics of Reservation Policy*. New Delhi: Patriot Publishers.

NAIR, A K K R (1986). *Slavery in Kerala.*, Delhi: Mittal Publications.

NISBET, R A (1966). *The Sociological Tradition*. New York: Basic Books.

O'HANLON, Rosalind (1985). *Caste, Conflict and Ideology. Mahatma Jotirao Phule and Low Caste Protest in XIX Century Western India.* Cambridge: Cambridge University Press.

PATEL, Tara (ed.) (1973). *Removal of Untouchability in Gujrat: A Seminar*. Ahmedabad: Gujarat University.

PIMPLEY P N, SHARMA S K (1986). *Struggle for Status*. Delhi: B.R. Publishing Corporation.

RAJYAGOR, S B (1977). *Gujarat State Gazetteers. Kheda District*. Ahmedabad: Government of Gujarat.

RAYAPPA P H, MUTHARAYAPPA, R, (1986). *Backwardness and Welfare of Scheduled Castes and Scheduled Tribes in India*. New Delhi: Ashish Publishing House.

RUDOLPH, L I, RUDOLPH, S H (1966). *The Modernity of Tradition: Political Development in India*. Chicago: University of Chicago Press.

SCHEIN, E H, BENNIS, W G (1965). *Personal Growth and Organizational Change through Group Methods: The Laboratory Approach*. New York: John Wiley.

SHAH, Ghanshyam (1984). *Economic Differentiations and Tribal Identity*. Delhi: Ajanta Publications.

SHARMA, K L (1986). *Caste, Class and Social Movements*. Jaipur: Rawat.

SHETH, D L (1979). "Politics of Caste Conflict" in *Seminar*, No. 233, January 1979.

SHOWEB, M (1986). *Education and Mobility among Harijans*. Allahabad: O.P. Vora Publications.

SINGH, R G (1986). *The Depressed Classes of India*. Delhi: B.R. Publishing Corporation.

SINGH, Soran (1987). *Scheduled Castes of India. Dimensions of Social Change*. Delhi: Gian Publishing House.

SINGH, Yogendra (1980). *Social Stratification and Change in India*. New Delhi: Manohar Book Service.

SINHA R K (1986). *Alienation among Scheduled Castes*. Delhi: Manas Publications. [A study of the village Khurja in Bulandshahr, U.P.]

SMITH, W A (1976). *The Meaning of Conscientizacao: The Goal of Paulo Freire's Pedagogy*. Amherst, Mass.: Center for International Education. University of Massachusetts.

SPODEK, Howard (1975). "Sardar Vallabhbhai Patel at 100" in *Economic and Political Weekly*, X, 50: 1925-36.

SRINIVAS, M N (1962). *Caste in Modern India*. Bombay: Asia Publishing House.

THERBORN, Goran (1980). *The Ideology of Power and the Power of Ideology*. London: Verso/NLB.

WEERAMAN, P E (1971). "Law and the Cooperative Movement" in *State and Cooperative Development*. Bombay: Allied Publishers.

INDEX

Afforestation, 46, 70
Agricultural
    Cooperatives historical
        development of 47-51
    productivity, 38
    technology, 6
Agriculture, 45-46
    expenditure on, 75
Alienation, 50
Animal health care, 129-132
Awareness, 105-107

Backward class, 7
Behavioural Science Centre, 1-17
Bhal, 18-19
Bhangis, 22, 91
Bharwads, 27, 29, 84-85
Bonded labourer, 39
Breeding, 134

Cambay, 18
Capitalism
    transcendence of, 50
Caste conflicts, 26-29, 86-95
Caste ideology, 9-17, 40, 114-124
    evils of 124-125
    qualification and, 119-120
Caste people, 95-96
Caste system
    as ideology, 114-116
Catholic conversion movement, 31-32
Catholic Relief Services, Bombay, 81
Chamars, 22
Charcoal manufacturing, 82-83
Christianity, 31-32
Common ownership, 53-55, 58-59
Communication, 69
Consciousness, 121-123
Cooperative movement, 41-51
    achievements of, 64-83
    historical development of, 47-51

ideology of, 51-58
successes of, 58-63
Cooperatives, 6, 64-65t
    as business enterprise, 77-83
    centre and, 98-104
    Control over
        types of, 56-58
    democratic set up in, 61-62
    grants received by
        village-wise, 76
    ideological trends in, 49-51
    income & expenditure of, 79-82
    individuals control over, 60-61
    investments in
        village-wise 74-76
    loans given to, 74-76
    means of production
        control of, 54-55, 60-62
        ownership 53-54, 58-59
    as new social structure 72-73
    ownership and, 53-54, 58-62
    socio-economic goals of, 73-77
    tasks of, 71
    technical education and, 70-72
    technological change, 52-53, 58
    as universities, 110-112
    variety of, 49

Desai, I.P., 21
Development,
    meaning of, 105-112
Divide and rule, 12
Dushkin, jelah, 20

Economic conditions,
    influence of, 105-106
Economic self-sufficiency scheme, 40-42
    see also Cooperative movement
Economic structure, 73-77
Education, 2
    purpose of, 15